LOCALISM DEFENDED

The Narrow Path between Anarchy and the Central State

By Mark M. Moore

Third Edition, Copyright 2015

The Ridge Enterprise Group

ISBN: 978-0-9962390-0-4

Table of Contents

Continued on next page

Purposes and Premises

"The natural progress of things is for liberty to yield, and government to gain ground." - Thomas Jefferson to Edward Carrington, Paris, May 27, 1788

The original work *Localism, A Philosophy of Government* was mostly prescriptive. That is, it defined the philosophy and described the thirteen doorways to centralization that any nation which hopes to remain free must shut, and further suggested how they might best be kept shut. It did not attempt to defend the philosophy from charges and attacks by advocates of other philosophies of government.

For most of the political spectrum, there is little need to do so. Localism is simply a framework by which power is kept decentralized. It is an effort to counter the effect Jefferson was referring to when he wrote to Edward Carrington "*The natural progress of things is for liberty to yield and government to gain ground.*"

Who could object to a framework which merely insures government power is dispersed and therefore kept within reach of the *individual* citizen? Who could object to a philosophy which leaves people in different places free to decide for themselves, within the limits of a Republic, what is or is not done with such power? Well, as it turns out there are two categories of complainants who have aired several would-be objections to the philosophy.

As the ideas behind localism have spread, so too has opposition to the philosophy. I rise to defend it, but the great advantage of localism is that I need not refute all other ideas on government in order to do so. Unless the reader is in one of two camps, I need not convert them out of their present views on the subject of government, but merely induce them to incorporate what *Localism* offers in a way which very likely dovetails with ideas which they may already hold.

Localism is more like a "meta-philosophy" of government, leaving room for many other ideas within it. Localism does not have to prove that all other philosophies of government are invalid or unjust in order to "win". People who hold other ideas are even freer to try them out in a localist society than they would be under a central state of any sort, because under a central state only one philosophy of government can "win" at a time.

I do not believe that all philosophies of government will fare equally well under localism though, because localism is all about applying the free market to government. I want to be clear- I do not mean that in the sense it is sometimes used where one pushes for "privatization" of government functions. That often results in cronyism, the opposite of a true free market. I mean to apply the free market to government itself in the sense of *individuals* having choice of government.

In economic terms, in various ways localism lowers the "transaction costs" of removing oneself out from under the authority of a government which one dislikes. The market will thereby reward those local governments which operate fairly and efficiently. It will swiftly punish those which do not. This will not come about because there will be words on paper specifying government is to be "fair". We have all seen how governments can ignore and twist such words. Rather this will occur naturally as the costs of either leaving government authority, or rebuking those running it, comes within reach of the individual citizen.

For a true free market to work, both costs and benefits must accrue to the consumer in order to establish their real preferences. This has not occurred under the central state, because the central state has at its disposal several strategies to conceal or shift the true costs of its growth. This conundrum gave rise to the famous quote of Frederic Bastiat that "G*overnment is the great fiction by which everybody endeavors to live at the expense of everybody else.*"

It's time to end the fiction. Localism's provisions prevent the sort of games government has played vis-a-vi concealing its true costs. Cost shifting is easy under a central-state model. It is difficult to impossible when the bill cannot be sent to the next generation via federal debt, or sent to the distant residents of another region. In Localism the furthest the bill can be sent is to one's neighbors, who will simply leave if they decide that the bill is too high.

The market will thus quickly punish those forms of governance which are farthest from moral reality. The worst forms will be both easier to change and easier to escape under localism, and thus go extinct in favor of more just forms. We find that freedom can work on its own merits. It is tyranny which must have a captive audience.

Localism can be considered merely a system for providing structural integrity and protection to "containers of government." The people of each state and county, or even city or township in some cases, decide for themselves what sort of government to put into these containers. Because it does not insist on "one right answer" to most questions about what the rules should be, localism is centrist. Because it is halfway between the concepts of a strong central state and no state at all, it is centrist. It is a "moderate" position in the best possible sense of the word. Opposition to a position that is truly centrist and moderate then, must come from the extremes.

This is what we see. What kinds of people oppose localism? Extremists oppose localism. And since there are two extremes there are two kinds of opposition. One extreme is an expansive central state where all the rules for the nation are basically made by the elite in one city. I consider that an extreme position, but unfortunately it reflects what we have now in the United States and in other Western nations. Therefore, defenders of the *status quo*, failure though it may be for most of the country, are also advocates of this sort of extremism.

The fact that the all-powerful central state, stuffed full of central planners managing our lives for us from afar, is currently ascendant does not in any way change the fact that it is an extreme position. We in the West do not currently have a moderate form of government. We have an extreme one, where power is *extremely* centralized. America did not start out with an extreme form of government. America began as a nation where power was quite *de*centralized. Localism is not a new idea. It is merely a re-birth and logical extension of the ideas which first produced the American Experiment.

Unfortunately, since the founding each fifty year span of time ended with the American Republic saddled with a more powerful and expansive central government than it had during the previous fifty year time period. We were not formed as a nation with an extremist form of government, rather we became one. As Jefferson noted, liberty tends to yield, and government tends to gain ground.

So one place opposition is found to localism is from those extremists who advocate for a strong central state. Some of them are not adamant in their extremism however. They are "conservative" in the "opposed to change" sense of the word. Their commitment to our present circumstances run no deeper than the idea that we have a central state now, so let's keep having one. This group is not really committed to big government as much as they are fearful of change.

Others want a strong central government because they are somehow connected to this system. They make money off of it by various means, more money than their talents and energies could gain them in a true free market. As such they are protecting their means of gain. And then there are the true believers.

The true believers are those groups who are currently exercising power over the rest of us (the ruling class) or those who hope to be. These people are sincerely convinced that they know the right answers to every question for everybody to the point that they are willing to force those answers on the bulk of the population whether that population agrees with them or not.

Our present politics consists of numerous groups fighting for control of the one gun to be pointed at the rest of us. It is a battle for "the ring of power." In Localism there is no one ring. There is no one gun and the vast multitude of little guns have too short a range to hold people captive unless they choose to be.

What advocates of Localism see as a benefit, the would-be gun-pointers see as a threat. They want all the rules made from one throne, because they just can't let go of the idea that someday, they and their friends may occupy that throne. Localism is for people who can sleep well at night even though people they have never met in a city where they have never been are doing things differently. Some are not at peace with that concept.

The short-hand way of describing these "true-believers" in central power is that they are elitists. Naturally most elitists see themselves as a part of the elite. They know how people they have never met in cities where they have never been in ought to live, and they can't wait around for those strangers to figure it out for themselves!

The elitist mind-set is not limited to those currently in power. Outsider groups can still see themselves as the ones who ought to be running things. Thus they will have a preference for a strong central state, since they one day hope to seize control of its machinery in order to impose their will on the rest of the populace.

So leftist college professors might be part of the "true believer" statists, and so might some stains of religious conservatives. Opposition to localism is not defined by, and largely not even applicable to, the conventional left-right political spectrum. Rather it is determined by one's place on the up-down spectrum. This up-down spectrum has a totalitarian central state at one end and anarchy at the other. Localism is in the middle, advocating neither the expansive central state nor the absence of state.

This brings us to the second "extreme" from whence opposition to the philosophy of localism has emerged. That is from the far end of the libertarian spectrum called "anarchists" or sometimes "anarcho-capitalists" or even "voluntaryists." Older readers may wonder why so much of this book will be dedicated to addressing the arguments of a faction of a libertarian movement which is itself small compared to statists. Younger readers will know why. Various flavors of the anarchist position have gained adherents among the young all out of proportion to its success in the real world. This position is a reaction to the increasingly evident abuses and weaknesses of the central state and the obvious failure of central planning.

A growing number of people are starting to wonder if mankind would not just be better off with no government at all. Many of them see government itself as downright immoral. To them, government is not a powerful tool which can be misused, rather they believe it is inherently wrong. That is the view at the other extreme of the up-down political spectrum. It is an extreme position, but it is one that is gaining a lot of ground. I suspect that many who read this book will do so for what it has to say about the case for government, in particular government which goes beyond the non-aggression principle.

Of course, being at one 'extreme' end of a spectrum does not necessarily mean that a position is wrong. I may believe that *those* extreme positions are wrong, at least while humanity is in its current state, but they are not wrong because they are extreme. They are wrong because they are out of tune with moral reality given who and what man is. More on that as we go. The bottom line is that Localism is the moderate position, one that is much closer to the ideals on which America was founded, and it is opposed by the extremes of centralized government power and no government at all.

Unbalanced Political Philosophies Regarding Public vs. Private Threats to Liberty

"If men were angels, no government would be necessary. If angels were to govern men, neither external nor internal controls on government would be necessary." - James Madison in the Federalist #51

Almost everyone agrees that a valid function of government is to protect individual rights. Indeed some would consider this to be the primary or even the solitary legitimate function of government. Even people who have different ideas about what one's "rights" are, or what the outer limits of how they ought to be exercised might be, can still agree that protecting the rights of the individual is a valid function of government.

Those on the far anarchist/voluntaryist end of the spectrum might say that it is the persistent tendency of government to abuse and move beyond this solitary function which makes government's existence more trouble than it is worth! Yet even they would say that if a government has any business at all existing, it would be to protect individual rights.

While the rise of the post-modern central state has shown the state itself to be the biggest threat to the rights which it is supposed to protect, this does not mean that if there were no government at all that violations of our individual rights would vanish altogether. Rather, it would mean that private threats to our rights would gain a freer hand.

There are two sources of threats to individual rights- Public Threats and Private Threats. Public Threats to rights include government oppression (frequently in cahoots with private interests). Private Threats are threats to individual rights which are either illegal under the law of your government or actions taken without the approval of your government, i.e. - crime or invasion from outside groups, including other governments.

Which category of threat seems the largest to someone is largely a function of their environment. If you live among genteel and intellectual types in Suburbia or small-town USA, you likely have known little of the gross deprivation of rights which is suffered from Private Threats in areas where there has been a break-down of civil government. If you are such a person, then you likely have the freedom and intellect and curiosity to take note of the ongoing, serious, and systemic Public Threats to individual rights. To you, Public Threats are the greatest and most immediate danger.

Realistically, there is presently no serious Private (extra-legal) threat to your liberties from a foreign government if you live in America. We have been the lone super-power in the world for at least 30 years. If your age of "awareness" was after that time you have not even known such a threat in your adult life. Many of us are surrounded by people who are prosperous enough so that they don't have to rob and steal in order to survive, and by habit and moral training would resist such an inclination anyway.

Though we are not exactly angels, it is easy to see why, from such a viewpoint, it would seem as though no government would be necessary. If we live in a nice neighborhood, protected from external Private Threats by a vast yet distant military, and surrounded by other individuals like ourselves who are not much of a Private Threat, then we might not see government as protecting us from anything. Rather it could be reasonably viewed as the most likely immediate threat to our freedoms.

My point is that if you come from such an environment you are likely to understate the risk of Private Threats to our liberties, and develop a philosophy of government which reflects that deeply affected risk assessment. If you live in Somalia or inner city Detroit, you see a general breakdown of government. Private Threats to your individual rights would abound. Private gangs, not government gangs, do the most robbing and killing in such places. A person in that situation would be more like almost all persons were before the rise of the modern central state- one who viewed Private Threats as a great danger and government power as a protector and defender of individual rights.

Ultimately, a moral population will not need much government. They have little use for it. For an immoral population, even a harsh and repressive central government might protect rights better than having no government at all. Thus the best defense against big government is a virtuous population.

The closer men get to angels, the less they need rulers. But for right now, we live in a world with both good and bad people, and where even usually good people can do bad things. We live in a world where there are both Public and Private Threats to liberty. One or the other may seem dominant to you, depending on your life experience and view of history, but either threat can become the dominant one depending on the ebb and flow of one's circumstances and public morality. A workable philosophy of government is one that accounts for both Public and Private Threats.

Localism is the balanced position. That is, it is in the center. From there it can defend against the loss of individual rights which tend to occur when either of the two extremes rule a society. The extreme statism currently practiced by central governments around the world leads to various sorts of Public Threats to individual rights. The extreme anarchist position, if it ever became the norm, would enable a massive and gross increase in Private Threats. This is what happens now when all but the most decent and civil people on earth are without government. Anarchy creates conditions where most people cry out for even a dictator. They will accept a loss of freedom for the promise of restored order!

I am a Localist because this is the philosophy which best avoids the threats to human rights posed by the extremist positions of the state-ists and the self-ists. Men are not angels, thus they need government, but government is run by men, so government too must be restrained and restricted. Maximum liberty is preserved when government exists but is limited by several means, including geography and the marketplace.

Generational Differences in Perception of Public vs. Private Threats

In the previous chapter I gave an example of the profile of a person who would tend to understate Private Threats to our rights relative to Public Threats. This misperception might lead them to be sympathetic toward a philosophy of government which was out-of-balance. That is to say it might lead them to a philosophy which would believe in reducing civil government to such an extent that it could not adequately protect people from Private Threats.

That is half the story, but there is also a typical profile of people who tend to take the opposite view- they understate Public Threats and overstate the need for a strong central state in order to protect against alleged Private (extra-legal) threats to freedom. A key demographic difference in the two views is age.

There is a vast generation gap which exists concerning the question of 'what is America?" The older generation sees America as a force for good around the world and throughout its history. And by "America" they mean both the actual country and its government. There was an expression that was around when I was growing up, "America, Love it or Leave it". That describes the attitude pretty well. They may not trust one of the two DC-based political parties who pick our leaders, but they cheer on the other with a full-throttled enthusiasm normally reserved for sports teams. The idea that America could be in the wrong is very disturbing to them. Their default position is that America is good.

The truth is that America has done good deeds. She has also done evil. Her actions are not inherently good just because she is America. Nor are they inherently evil. Instead, as with all of us as individuals, when they are good they are good, and when they are bad they are bad.

Remember that the older generation in this country was raised in a very different "Private Threat" environment than the younger generation. They were fresh off of WWII, where the Japanese bombed Pearl Harbor and the Germans had fallen under the spell of an aggressive and deeply flawed personality. America was "the arsenal of Democracy." We used our strong central state to preserve freedom against militaristic dictatorships.

This effort continued in the Cold War. Today's older generation were raised in a time when it seemed that the Communist block was a legitimate threat to bring the rest of the world under heel. To a younger reader sitting in the safety of our current military strength, these fears may seem comical, but then again, they were there, you weren't.

The conditioning and experiences of the older generation make them very susceptible to being whipped up into a frenzy over perceived threats from "terrorists". "The Islamic Threat" was discounted by many younger Americans as being ridiculously over-blown, and merely a pretext to expand government control and power over the people. I tend to agree, but then younger Americans have not been conditioned to think of our Federal Government as the Great Protector against powerful Private Threats to our freedom. Older Americans have been so conditioned. "The War on Terror" was time for them to rally 'round their country again, as they had done before from childhood.

The older generation has been conditioned to accept such threats as so real, and the role of our central government as so helpful in defending them, that they were easy pickings for the propagandists in the Beltway. They were much more likely than younger Americans to accept or support the growth of the police-state which we have recently seen. Their life-training tended to make them view these alarming trends as necessary measures from a well-meaning central government which had protected us from such threats before.

It is also generally true that older Americans are more fearful of crime than younger Americans. Since they do tend to be more prosperous, they are a more attractive target for Private Threats against their liberties, such as criminals. This is at a time of life when their own physical ability to protect themselves and their families is waning. This leads them quite naturally to view a strong police presence as a good thing. They long for security in a way that younger Americans might not understand. They grew up before the militarization of the police, in an era of "Officer Friendly." Their perceptions of present are affected by their experiences of the past.

Remember too that over a lifetime they had been trained to see the central government as competent managers of the nation's economic prosperity. The nation experienced decades of apparent economic prosperity until fairly recently. The younger generation sees the stagnation and debt that is our present.

The older generation was coaxed into accepting the idea that our federal government had a duty to "stimulate the economy". In essence the federal government seemed to successfully solve problems (which were caused by their previous policies) by government "pump-priming". Never mind that their apparent multi-decade success was actually an illusion manufactured by the issuing of what amounts to trillions of dollars of "hot checks". That is, debt which poorer younger Americans are now somehow expected to pay.

So the older generation tends to understate Public Threats to liberty and overstate Private Threats. People who do that will gravitate towards a political philosophy which reflects this flawed perception. "Neoconservative" and "Big Government Conservative" are two terms which have been used to describe the political philosophy which results from such perception imbalances, but the older term for it is fascism. There are many Americans walking around today who consider themselves "conservatives" who are actually much closer to fascists. The same goes for some who call themselves "liberals."

Ironically, people who first appreciated a strong central government because it defended America against fascism have nearly come full circle, and are unknowingly near to embracing the philosophy from which they initially sought protection. But those experiences defending the nation against Private Threats are not the sole, and maybe not the biggest, reason for the generational divide in viewpoints. It comes also from the way people were educated in prior generations.

It has been said that the state will not hesitate to use public education to further its political goals. The goal of the leaders of prior generations was to convince the populace that the country was good and its policies benevolent. That's what the public schools taught, and that's what the population believed. But the people who controlled the school system changed goals sometime in the 1960s or 1970s (though implementation of those goals took decades and is on-going). They had a different agenda. They wanted citizens with a global, rather than a national, outlook. They wanted to de-emphasize American patriotism and American religion (Christianity). They were early examples of today's globalists.

With this new goal, the schools no longer taught that America was a beacon on a hill, an unmitigated force for good to whom all the world should look for guidance. Instead they went to the other extreme. Education emphasized the things America did that were wrong. They focused on actions we took which were inconsistent with our own ideals. Was it America bashing, or just correcting a previous imbalance toward a sort of patriotism which never questioned government action? I am not writing to decide that huge question, but rather the effects of this change. It has resulted in a vast generation gap on the question of "is America good?"

The younger generation is quick to believe that America is in the wrong. So quick that I would estimate that a majority of 17-24 year old Americans with an opinion on the matter believe that 9/11 was an inside job perpetrated by the government to incite popular support for a global military campaign abroad and an expanding police state at home. Almost no one over sixty believes that. The younger generation does not believe the government story about the JFK assassination, or almost anything else. They have been trained to be distrustful of all authorities, because they were being educated to reject the values and attitudes of their parents, their church, and their national institutions.

The globalists got much of what they wanted in reprogramming the next generation, but their plan may have some unforeseen consequences that they won't like. This campaign against traditional authorities worked, but it is now starting to boomerang back on its creators. The globalists are now the authorities, and the younger generation does not trust them anymore than the authority figures they have been educated to mistrust. The young have been trained to believe in nothing, and so they don't even believe those who trained them! That spiritual vacuum can't last long, because the human heart is not made to live that way.

But the bottom line is that young people are turning to anti-authoritarian icons like Ron Paul, despite the desperate attempts of the establishment to paint Paul as a nut. The globalists wanted to tear down traditional sources of authority in order to make way for themselves as the replacement. In terms of power, it's working, but it's not turning out that way "hearts and minds" wise. A generation trained to doubt the good intentions of every authority only want to give authority to people who are anti-authoritarian. Many reject the very concept of government authority.

The Progress of the Book

People are individuals, and it is often a mistake to judge an individual based on the statistics of their demographic. Still, in general one can make statements about demographics that it would be unfair to apply to individuals within them. In the last two chapters we have explored the two extreme viewpoints with which localism is not compatible, and laid the groundwork for our case that flawed perceptions about the relative danger of Public vs. Private threats are at the core of both extremes.

Two chapters previously, I gave an example of the sort of person who would tend to understate Private Threats to liberty relative to Public Threats to liberty. The philosophy of government which is the logical conclusion of that misperception is called Anarchism. Notice that the logic behind the philosophy can still be correct, but if such logic is based on flawed premises the conclusion from the correct logic can still be wrong.

In the last chapter I focused on the sort of person who would tend to understate Public Threats to liberty relative to Private Threats. The philosophy of government which is the logical conclusion of that misperception is Statism or Fascism, though it is not so often called the latter because such philosophies are uncomfortably close to the present *status-quo*. Again, one does not have to be illogical to be a supporter of a strong central government while believing in liberty, but it does reflect a faith in human masters not supported by the evidence. In other words, it too is operating from a flawed premise.

These two flawed premises are the polar opposites of one another. One is that individuals are good enough to be entrusted with their own government, the other is that they can't be so entrusted, but that some elite group from among them can be entrusted to run the lives of people from afar better than those people can do so themselves. At times, both viewpoints are right and both are wrong. It is a paradox.

Localists understand the problem expressed by Madison when he wrote "*If men were angels, no government would be necessary. If angels were to govern men, neither external nor internal controls on government would be necessary.*"

Men are not angels. Even the best of us are capable of bad things. And even if some of us were angels, we would need protection from those of us who were not. We need government, but since that government is itself composed of men who at times cannot or will not govern themselves according to the moral order of the angels, then those men who run government need controls placed on them too, both external and internal.

Our founders, in recognition of this truth of human nature, devised a Republic where certain agreed-on rights were recognized to be outside the reach of government and most especially the central government. They instituted a nation where the central government was limited to only a few functions, with the rest left to the states or to the people. Their model worked beautifully, failing only to stop the process Jefferson warned about: Over time, liberty yielded and government gained ground. It would make for a better world if the reverse were true. Localism attempts to build a framework for a nation in which the reverse will be true.

This book will be divided into three further sections. One defends the Philosophy against Anarchist Arguments. I do not bother to distinguish here between "Anarchist" and "Voluntaryist" labels because in terms of the philosophical foundations of government the distinctions between the two are not large enough to matter. They both reject the necessity of external government for human civilization and share basically the same premises for doing so. The next section of the book will contend against the statists. Then there will be a brief conclusion.

Different Kinds of Libertarians

This book is about a philosophy of government which values decentralization, and therefore tolerance of a wide variety of viewpoints on what government should be and do. Most forms of Libertarian thought, ironically, do not share that value. From that quarter, there is only one correct set of premises from which one ought to reason about human government. From these limited premises come narrow conclusions. Much of the volume of this work will be devoted to showing why such assumptions are, if not wrong, at least not *necessarily* correct.

With that being said, Localism is quite compatible with most minarchist Libertarian ideas about government, so long as one is not insistent that these ideas be imposed on areas of the nation where they have little support. There has been some misunderstanding about this based on the final chapter of the previous book.

The final chapter in *Localism, A Philosophy of Government* did express skepticism for the idea that government which was strictly limited to enforcing the Non-Aggression Principle (NAP) would result in optimal law- that is, law which was most in accordance with moral reality. This skepticism though, was meant to steer readers away from a "one size fits all" way of looking at things, not a rejection of minarchist Libertarian government as a possible outcome of a localist nation. This quote, from the final chapter of the book, sums it up...

"But perhaps you are a libertarian who is not persuaded by my rhetoric. You should support localism just the same. Localism is the best shot you will have at getting your libertarian society. Additionally, it is the escape hatch you might need to undo that society should it be less utopian in reality than on paper. Can you imagine trying to undo it under a centralized government where those in the distant capitol, whose whole privileged position is based on their loyalty to enforcing the libertarian absolute as they see it, are the last to acknowledge that their theories don't work out?

If libertarianism is correct, in localism it can triumph one locality at a time. Those who wish to flee to it may do so, and if enough wish it they might even bring their cities to you. If it is not correct, or even if it is but some wish not to choose it, then they are free to do so."

That final chapter was written as an appeal to minarchists to take a Localist route to a libertarian society. It was not a claim that the philosophy was somehow disqualified from consideration, but rather pointing out the advantages of building such a government within a localist framework.

One advantage, made clear throughout the book, but not in this passage, is that a minarchist state without the safeguards enumerated in Localism does not have the means to resist the growth in centralized power which ultimately results in its undoing. That is, libertarians should support a localist framework for their minarchist state because such a state will not be sustained without it.

That a minarchist state eventually becomes something more oppressive than a minarchist state is one of the main charges anarchists level against minarchists. Unlike some of their claims, those regarding the tendency of minimalist governments to grow into something more over time is very well documented in the pages of history. Minarchy within a localist framework addresses this valid criticism.

Another advantage of minarchist libertarians pursing their goals in a localist framework is that Libertarian ideas can triumph, if indeed they are the best way of doing things, state by state in Localism. That is, one might pursue minarchist goals in one's own state without people in other states who might object to it having a say in the matter. It is much easier to convince people to change things in a manner which will allow them to decide the rules where they live than it is to convince them all to change things in a way so that only one set of rules is considered everywhere.

By such a strategy libertarian minarchy can be achieved in states which are eager for it while one waits for the others to "catch up." And of course, just as it is easier for states to achieve a more libertarian condition under localism, so it is easier for them to move out of it if for some reason it is found to be less complete and just in reality than it is in theory.

So while I personally don't see the Non-Aggression Principle (NAP) as an all-inclusive moral code relative to government authority, it is also clear that those who do could still mostly have their way under localism. Libertarians come in many forms. Because the label is becoming trendy, there are many people who claim it who do not take an absolutist approach to the idea that government should be strictly limited to the NAP. Some of these people might be better defined as "Constitutionalists" or even localists who don't (yet) know it.

Even among those "pure" libertarians who see the NAP as the be-all end-all basis for legitimate government action, we find that localism could work well with a libertarian view. The central government in localism is merely a subset of even a minarchist libertarian government, needing help from the states to complete even those functions. It is then up to each state to decide if they wish to stop at the minarchist model or if they believe that there are further justifications for government action. County flexibility is another safeguard.

So then libertarians might be classed into three broad groups. The first and perhaps largest group are the "soft" libertarians who don't view the Non-Aggression Principle in absolutist terms. To them the Non-Aggression Principle is just that, a Principle. A principle is something which is generally true, but to which there are exceptions. Then there are the "Pure" or "Hard" libertarians who see the NAP as a Law- a law being something which is always true and to which there are no exceptions.

These hard libertarians are divided into two categories. The one category then is minarchists (the soft libertarians usually fall here as well) which believe that one can justly have a government for the enforcement of the NAP. The other category stands in opposition to them all. These are the anarchists or voluntaryists (for brevity I shall henceforth lump the two together) who maintain that there should be nothing like we would consider government at all.

With that made clear, let it be said that it is the anarchists, who tend to be highly critical even of the other two groups of libertarians, who are the ones whose philosophy is not *ultimately* compatible with localism. Even some of them however, see it as a way station or intermediate point whereby government power is reduced in geographic scope until ultimately it falls to the individual, at which point anarchy is achieved.

I appreciate this view, since it inclines them favorably to localism, but in all honesty the philosophy rests on very different premises and this will lead to very different outcomes. This is so not only in terms of final destination (for example, whether one should favor reducing government from the county to the township to the household to the individual) but also in terms of what decisions ought to be made along the way.

Since the central state is now ascendant, Localists are walking in the same direction as anarchists, but we are both walking on the same path towards decentralization for our own reasons, and with the intentions of reaching a different destination. We are walking toward the center from the one extreme position of the central state and wish to stop in the middle ground of the decentralized state. Anarchists wish to keep marching off towards the other edge. While on the way together, it never hurts to dialog. Perhaps by the time we get to the place where we plan to part company one or the other traveler will have a change of heart.

Other anarchists lash out at localism with the same ferocity they seem use against all that is not anarchism. They are one of the "extremes" which I discussed earlier. In the sections which follow, I will defend Localism from attacks based on Anarchist premises. Some of this must necessarily bleed over into the NAP. This is not done to show the premises behind the NAP are *necessarily* false, for localism can accommodate forms of government which accept the NAP as true. Rather, the goal is to show that other reasonable premises might also be true. This includes premises which indicate that the NAP, while perhaps a good principle (which is to say something that is generally true), should not be treated as a law (something that is always true without exception) with respect to the limits of civil government.

While I am going to defend the validity of government against anarchist premises, let everything I say in the next seventy or eighty pages be tempered by this: Right now what we have is an extreme central state. Anarchists want to go all the way over to the other extreme, while localists want to move most of the way over, enough so that the market can make government accountable. We may fight over where we should stop, but we should not have to fight over the direction we should be going. Breaking political units down into smaller sizes should be something favored by anarchists because it brings them closer to their ultimate goal of breaking it all the way down to the individual.

If society can move, if we make progress, then we should be riding the same train for the next 1,000 miles. During that time we should have a civil discussion about the validity and certainty of each of our premises. We can talk about how much government should be decentralized. Perhaps a localist would say that local governments in voluntary associations called states, and states in voluntary associations called nations, is the proper level of decentralization. Thus the standard is that association between local governments and all higher governments is voluntary.

The anarchist would go further and say "government" should be decentralized all the way down to the individual. They would say that not just localities should have all relationships on a voluntary basis, but each person should. It sounds good, but is it really workable? Will it really produce a better, and freer society?

We can have those debates. We can talk about whose premises are the soundest. But in the course of scrutinizing one another closely, let's not forget that the real mutual opponent is the centralizers. It is those who would take decision-making over your life further from you, not we who would bring it nearer. Localists are only the "enemies" of anarchists when and if we win. Right now, we both have some real oppression to worry about.

On Atheists and Religious Fanatics

"There are more things in heaven and earth, Horatio,
Than are dreamt of in your philosophy." – Hamlet

"Those who never retract their opinions love themselves more than they love truth." – Joseph Joubert

"It is the mark of an educated mind to be able to entertain a thought without accepting it." - Aristotle

People can talk past one another, even if both are using sound logic, if they start from different premises. Sadly, I have seen numerous attempts at dialogue, even between logical people, thwarted because at least one party was unable or unwilling to examine a question from any premises other than the ones which they themselves held. I don't mean here reasoning from a demonstrably false premise, but simply from one with which the thinker does not agree even though it cannot be either proven or disproven by the debaters.

Unfortunately, human beings are forced to reason from premises which they cannot verify in a strict scientific sense. For example, does God exist? Very different things become reasonable or unreasonable just based upon the answer to that one question, but sages, scientists, and philosophers have debated the answer to that one question for ages.

Many of the arguments presented in the following pages are based on the idea that God does exist. Though this book should make perfect sense to agnostics and believers alike, I don't think the approach used here will do any good with someone so bound by their own skin as an atheist.

One must be able to “get outside themselves” in order to understand a position based on a premise which the thinker rejects. This is to say they must be able to do what Aristotle said was the mark of an educated mind. A committed atheist is unlikely to be able to free themselves of themselves enough to do this. Were they able to do so, surely they would not maintain a position which they could not possibly have enough information to reasonably hold.

The atheist claims that there is no god, anywhere in the universe or beyond it. They have of late, been crab-walking away from this definition of the term, but whether one dismisses the existence of God or simply the possibility that there might be legitimate evidence for the existence of God, the end result is much the same. Such a person must hold that each and every other person throughout human history who has claimed they have experienced God in some way must be either lying or mistaken.

Again, they would have no way to access even a fraction of the information required to support such a position. They do not have the ability to thoroughly evaluate even one percent of such claims. Yet this lack of knowledge does not seem to hinder them from asserting their conclusion. This inability to see outside of one's own skin is not a rational position, therefore a work which uses reason as its primary instrument will not be appealing.

The hard core atheist shares some of the same mental handicaps as the hard core religious fanatic. Neither can accept that there might be valid information about God out there somewhere that is contradictory to the position which they hold. They know it all, therefore there is no need to consider any other answer to the important questions. In their view, the answer is clear, even if it requires they do something which is clearly impossible for them- such as prove a pan-cosmological negative. For this type of mind, and the two are closer in profile than one might at first believe, there is only one possible right answer to the God question, and thus there is usually only one right answer to the government question.

The religious dogmatist is not necessarily the same as the religious fanatic. Given that God exists, and that humans can receive knowledge from the Divine as a gift, there is nothing unreasonable about a dogma. In spite of this, there is a certain human personality which masks their insecurity by using systems of religion to pretend there is no uncertainty in life. The thinking is that "if only one follows "X" rules rigidly enough then God will invariably cause "Y" result to follow."

To such closed minds, Localism, with its emphasis on free association and market-driven choices, is completely pointless. In their own view, they know the one right way for everyone. There is only one correct premise to reason from, and there is only one right place for the lines to be drawn- for everyone at all times. Their focus is on badgering everyone to do it the one "right way", not building a system which protects a variety of choices operating side by side with minimal friction.

Like so many atheists, they lack the ability to entertain positions which they do not hold. For both the atheist and the religious fanatic I have found that the root cause of this deficit is an out-of-balance personality. The imbalance manifests in one of two directions, either tending towards excessive arrogance which dismisses competing viewpoints without reflection on the one hand, and excessive fear and insecurity which dares not consider competing viewpoints on the other hand.

The rest of us see premises and the ideas which flow from them in three piles, not two. The premises we think are correct go in one pile, the premises that we don't think are correct but which we cannot prove wrong are in another, and then there are the ones we are convinced are wrong and wish to disallow. These folks lack that middle category which consists of the areas of life where we admit that, though we have our preferences, we just don't know the transcendent "right" answer, if there is one.

With that said, let's reason about that middle pile. When premises cannot be ruled out, correct reasoning from those premises cannot be ascertained to be true or untrue. They are possibly true. For example, if my premise it that red cars are more likely to get ticketed then I may reason that buying a car of another color will reduce my chances of getting a ticket. My reasoning may be correct, but until we have hard data on whether or not red cars get more tickets (and why) then we cannot determine if the purchase of a car of some other color, such as blue, will reduce one's chances of being ticketed. It is possibly true.

Ideas which are correctly reasoned from premises which we cannot disprove cannot be invalidated or shown to be wrong. They may or may not align with one's personal preferences, but unless one can show a flaw in the reasoning or falsify the premise from which the conclusion is derived, the idea is *possibly* true. Therefore, conclusions about government, correctly reasoned from reasonable premises which cannot be invalidated, should not be dismissed out of hand. They are possibly true.

One does not have to believe such conclusions. One may choose other premises from which to reason. But what harm is it to you if people you don't know in cities where you have never lived choose to order their society around a different view? This is a call for tolerance for a diversity of reasonable thought which is one of the hallmarks of localist philosophy.

Examining Self-Ownership

The Non-Aggression Principle and Self-ownership are often considered cornerstones of Libertarian and Anarchist thought, along with the idea of the Rule of Law. As a caveat, I recognize that not all libertarians consider Self-ownership to be an essential philosophical foundation of the creed- they would substitute other things such as the Principles of Delegation and Symmetry. I will address those substitute premises later. Self-ownership is considered foundational by many if not most libertarians, so let's talk about it first.

Here is the definition from Wikkipedia as of early 2014: *"Self-ownership (or sovereignty of the individual, individual sovereignty or individual autonomy) is the concept of property in one's own person, expressed as the moral or natural right of a person to have bodily integrity, and be the exclusive controller of his own body and life. According to G. Cohen, the concept of self-ownership is that "each person enjoys, over himself and his powers, full and exclusive rights of control and use, and therefore owes no service or product to anyone else that he has not contracted to supply."*

Self-ownership as described above sounds so reasonable, so "obvious" to the average westerner raised with post-modern premises that today's minds are quick to say "yes, of course that is true." It seems intuitively true to persons raised up immersed in a post-modern culture that we own ourselves.

This is why so many people, once they hear the idea expressed so plainly, immediately latch onto the concept and build their thoughts about government from there. The premise is typically not examined or evaluated prior to its adoption. Rather it is seized upon immediately as something which is *self-evidently true.* That is to say, it seems so clearly correct that it needs no outside supporting evidence to affirm it.

Advocates of the Principle of Self-ownership might be inclined to contemplate in wonder that it took mankind so long to formalize the proposition. They might ask "How did this idea, so self-evidently true, fail to occur to more persons in prior ages?" It is my experience though, that they usually don't even consider such a question. Perhaps they should.

One reason such a question is so seldom asked is because people today have been trained by the institutions which have shaped their thinking to have a dismissive view of the wisdom of prior ages. Somehow, all relevant wisdom is possessed by our own generation, while the ideas of prior generations accumulated over five thousand years of human civilization are cast aside as crude, silly, and unworthy of consideration.

Our ruling class and its media and institutions perpetuate this belief. Doing so has the effect of separating the population from wisdom and norms of prior ages against which the actions of the current ruling class might be evaluated. When all wisdom is held in the current age, then those ruling now need not be bound by admonitions from those who came before them. I believe that such arrogance is a grave mistake.

It is amazing how a few generations can change the way a culture looks at things. To many people today, the principle of Self-Ownership seems self-evidently true. Move back scarcely more than 250 years ago in the same culture. When the United States was founded a very different view, with different logical consequences, seemed "self-evident." For example the Declaration of Independence claimed that it was "self-evident" (so obvious to the observer of the day that it needed no proof or supporting facts) that men were "endowed by their Creator" with rights.

Notice that self-ownership or sovereignty of one's person was not the basis for the Declaration's claim that men have rights. The claim is not that men are sovereign. To the contrary, the claim is that men are a creation, and that as such it is their Creator, not their government, nor even their person, from which their freedom and dignity rightfully spring. Men have rights, not because they own themselves, but because their Creator granted them rights. To the culture of the day, this was just as self-evident as our culture's assumption (without contemplation) of self-ownership.

This different approach was not taken because our forebears were daft. It was not that the thinkers of the day failed to consider a possibility which is obvious to us now. They had considered the idea Self-Ownership even more than most people today who base their whole political philosophy around it. Consider Milton's classic *Paradise Lost.* A significant part of that work was examining what amounts to Self-Ownership as the premise held by the Devil. The great 1800s Scottish writer George McDonald, who wrote both books for children and works on Natural Law, once said "The first principle of Hell is 'I am my own.'"

Our forebears did not somehow fail to discover and examine the idea that we own ourselves and that our rights spring from our self-ownership. Rather, they examined the idea. They examined it more thoroughly than most today who claim it as their foundational premise. It wasn't that they didn't think of it. They did think if it and most then concluded that the concept was a flawed one.

Understand that I am not saying that the state owns us, nor am I saying that we own each other. There is at least one other possibility, and it is the classical position of the West for the last two-thousand years. I am amazed today that it is so overlooked, especially considering the view of Rights espoused in the Declaration of Independence. This is that we are the *steward* of our own life, and not (at least yet) its owner.

This position is that God owns us. This is both in terms of His right of ownership as the Creator for all mankind, and also for believers in terms of His salvation of our souls through the redemption of Christ ("you have been bought with a price" - 1 Corinthians 6). In this view, though He has placed us in this world and granted us much freedom to become who we want to be, before we are granted self-ownership we will be accountable to Him for the use we have made of that which we have been given.

So the classical view is that men are not the "owners" of our persons, but the *stewards* of our persons. We are not the sovereign, but we have authority from the Sovereign. Our authority is a derived authority granted by the Creator and rightful Sovereign of the universe. Our rightful authority then, if less sovereign than an anarchist might hope for, is at least far more legitimate than a state-worshipper might wish.

Under the classical western view not only are we stewards rather than owners, but our stewardship will be evaluated. Any "self" ownership we might have would come *after* Judgment day, once we as the stewards of our own lives have been evaluated on how we have done with what was entrusted to us.

I don't want to get into specific theology here, only that which was generally shared by all of Christendom, but I do want to make one important distinction which impacts our subject here: Man was not considered a moral neutral who had to decide between good and evil, God and the Devil. Rather he began as God's own, but due to rebellion and sin separated from God and joined the camp of rebellion. The decision of man then is not whether to choose one camp or the other from a morally neutral position, but rather whether he will leave the camp of rebellion and return to that of the Creator.

Self-ownership then is not something man currently possesses, but rather will be the result of judgment. One might even say that self-ownership is our judgment. For good or for ill, we will be given ownership of our lives. To some of us this will be a blessing, and for others a curse. In Hell no exterior law will be tolerated, in Heaven none will be needed. Which path you think produces freedom and which produces slavery is a matter of opinion determined by who you trust most-your own heart or God's. This idea is near the root of what is meant when Christians say that salvation is not by works, but by faith.

So the classical Western view is that the state does not own us, nor do we own ourselves, but both state and individual will be held accountable for how they act according to God's absolute moral order. We may not understand what "justice" means in a given situation, we may grope blindly about in the hard cases, but we are obligated to try. Rather than looking solely within to find justice, we are also to look out, and to look up. The state can, where allowed, judge the person for violations of this higher moral order and the person can, where allowed, judge the state for violations. Neither the individual nor the state is the absolute reference point for moral reality.

But let's get back more directly to the idea that we own ourselves. If I asked you why you thought you '"owned" your paycheck, you might say to me that your labor created the wealth that it represents. You might say that you made a voluntary agreement to exchange your efforts for the money, and that you lived up to your end of the bargain. That is, you performed the agreed-to work and have therefore earned the agreed-on price. You may be able to think of other good answers. But I can't help but notice that the reasons we might give to say that we "own" our paycheck cannot be applied to make the case that we own ourselves!

If you think about it, it's really hard to make the case that we "own ourselves." We did not create ourselves. We did not determine when or where we entered this world, and we do not get to decide whether or not we leave this world. Others did many things to us and for us- some with our permission, some without, which permitted us to reach adulthood. Each day a thousand things we cannot control in the heavens and on earth are necessary to sustain our lives. The idea that we are created, and in some sense accountable to our Creator, seems at least as rational a position as that of "self-ownership."

Again, I don't have to "prove" self-ownership is false, or that there is a Creator, nor I am trying to do that. Nor am I saying that the Non-Aggression Principle is a bad idea. I am simply showing that there are other possibilities about what it is or is not just for government to do. It is not so that there is "no intellectual case" for government beyond these ideas. Other conclusions are rational if one reasons from other premises. Among those other reasonable conclusions is that the Non-Aggression Principle is not necessarily the sole and absolute standard by which all actions, government and private, ought to be judged.

Unless advocates of Self-ownership can disprove these other premises, they cannot justly make the claim that their position on the limits of government action represent the only reasonable position. They may be the only reasonable conclusions from the premises which they hold, but others simply do not accept their premises. We hold other premises, ones which have historically produced a lot of human liberty and prosperity when we are able to restrain the state and our own hearts by them.

As I mentioned earlier, a much better case for "self-ownership" can be made in any eternal afterlife which might exist. There it might be argued that our place of entry *is* determined by our own choices, and that the being we have become is the result of our own choices. So while we may have had no hand in our own creation in this life, we would in the next. And the condition would be, unlike this world, permanent. What George McDonald called "the First Principle of Hell" makes sense as a reality in Hell. In this life, if God exists, we can only be as children in the womb, preparing for the next life but no more "sovereign" in this one than children yet unborn.

The concept of personal sovereignty, in the absolute sense Anarchists present it, implies each individual gets to determine their own morality. To be sure, they would prefer that all individuals adopt the NAP as the basis for morality, but if someone else adopts another standard, such as the strong should rule over the weak, or that the intelligent should rule the daft, one is hard pressed to find on what basis they might object, other than personal preference.

This is the inevitable result of any philosophy which declares each individual is a sovereign. In the Camp of Rebellion where each one asserts they are their own, even attempts to set limits to behavior based on the NAP will be accounted as a violation of their "sovereignty". Each rebel will have their own idea of what "principles" they consider "binding".

Again, measured against the vast scale of the cosmos, the enormity of time which has passed in all ages, and the value of wisdom which has endured for generations before us, the idea that the four pounds of gray matter in our skulls can be the sole and final arbiter of right and wrong, even for ourselves, seems at least open to reasonable dispute.

We can try and discern right from wrong, and a worthy life will spend time doing so, but this can be more reasonably seen as discovering the moral reality already present in the creation, not exercising some sort of sovereign power to manufacture one's own. The idea that each generation, and even more so each person, gets to re-write morality according to how they will it to be, from premises of their own choosing, does not seem any more legitimate than other ideas. At the least it is no more rational than the traditional idea that there *is* an absolute moral order to the universe, and we only get to discover it and either choose to conform to it or not. We don't, under the classical view, get to write our own.

Any one of us is only a tiny part of the natural world. We remain in it only an infinitesimal portion of the total time it has existed. The idea that we can construct our own personal morality and expect it to be honored by the rest of the world, displays what seems to me an almost psychotic misinterpretation of our place in the universe.

You may disagree, and that is fine. The point is, depending on our starting premises, either conclusion can be argued. Therefore, valid ideas about where government is allowed to act or not act which follow from those contradictory conclusions are also possible.

Seeing that this is so, why not support an approach which allows government to be constructed on each premise and let the results speak to which ideas produce the better society? Perhaps the better society will be different for different people. Why not let everyone win?

That is why I am a Localist. Instead of fighting over who gets to hold the single gun that is pointed at the rest of us from sea to shining sea, the central government would get no gun for enforcing moral imperatives, be that gun libertarian, socialist, conservative, liberal, or whatever.

States and localities would retain the power to sanction moral behavior such as mandating child support. But let them be careful how they use such power! For in such an arrangement states which go too far (that is, impose rules for moral behavior outside the underlying moral reality of the universe or beyond the legitimate scope of government compulsion) are bound to lose productive citizens to places which do not.

States and localities which did not go far enough would lose productive citizens too. And in each case government would look more like what the citizens who live there would want government to look like. Decentralizing power would make the government subject to the marketplace.

Disputing with Anarchists over Challenges to Self-Ownership

What follows is based on actual debates with Anarchists. The comments mirror objections from Anarchists who feel that Self-Ownership is the lynch-pin on which Liberty from tyrannical government depends. History shows that it is not. The Founders believed that God gave men liberty, and that His Justice demanded limits on the State and what it could do to its citizens. They had a different view for the basis for rights than is popular today. Still, this book is written to address objections raised to localist thought. One such objection comes from Anarchists, and is based on a certain view of self-ownership. I would like to re-create those objections and answer them here:

Anarchist: *I don't accept the existence of your god, or any god. I don't accept your view on self-ownership, therefore whatever rules your society chooses to enforce based on your beliefs about that cannot justly be applied to me. Society is wrong to put restrictions on my behavior based on what their belief is about some nebulous absolute moral order which I do not accept.*

Since you cannot force me to believe in your god without being a dictator, that means you cannot use the law to enforce a system which denies me self-ownership based on a deity having a higher claim to individual ownership. Because this system is impossible without the use of direct force against my wishes, my own claim over my life remains the highest legally enforceable under just law.

Localist: My logic stands whether God exists or not. If there is a God, and He does establish a moral order, you can be justly held accountable to that moral order whether you choose to believe in God or His moral order or not. Your belief in God is immaterial as to whether or not the sanction is just or unjust. If a higher moral order exists, your belief about whether the sanction is just or unjust is immaterial to its actual state of justice.

It is true that I cannot force you to believe in God against your wishes. Not even a dictator can do that, since belief is internal. However, I question your assertion that society cannot justly enforce a system which denies you self-ownership based on a deity having a higher claim on you. Society can claim a higher moral code which you can justly be made obligated to follow even if you don't view that code as binding on you. It is done all of the time. Our prisons are full of criminals who do not view society's laws, even the most just of them, as binding on them, for whatever reason.

The critical issue is whether or not the law is truly moral, not whether or not those it is being enforced against accept its morality. If there is a God, there is a moral order higher than that of created man. It may be that much of this moral order is not justly punishable by the state. I personally believe there are many things which are immoral, but which are outside the scope of the state to punish. But in those cases where an action is against the moral order, and the character of the action is such that it is justly punishable by the state, then the state may justly punish violations of the law regardless of whether or not those violating the law respect its validity. So in the case of God and the rest that follows, my logic stands.

But even if there is no creator God, my logic stands. If there is no god then there is no rational basis for individual liberty to be *morally* superior to rule by the Great Man. It may be one's personal preference, but that is not the same as moral imperative.

One may protest that "my own claim over my life remains the highest legally enforceable under just law", but without a source for a higher moral order there is no reference point to determine any one action any more "just" than any other. *Why* does one's claim of self-ownership trump the claim of someone smarter than you, or stronger than you, or who has their own needs or desires for something that you possess? On what basis does one then maintain that their claim is superior, or rather why aren't all claims equal and therefore meaningless?

Either there is a higher moral order or there is not. You are hopping between the moral relativism of a godless universe and the language of "rights" and "justice" which presuppose a transcendent moral law. And a moral law requires a Lawgiver.

What is material is the premise that God exists and that the sanction is in accordance with His moral code. I have not proven that here, but it was not my goal. My goal was to show that reason can produce different conclusions than Anarchist thought allows, and that this is so whether there is a God or not.

The key is that rational people can start reasoning from different premises. Some of these, like the classical Western views I espouse, are based on premises which cannot be disproved, and for which much historical evidence exists. The anarchist risks an angry existence experiencing little interpersonal growth if they dismiss all logical thought from others just because they choose another premise from which to reason. I say all that to make a call for tolerance if the people in the next state or the next county set up their society on premises different from those which we might hold.

But, again, and it is so important that I can't emphasize it enough, even if there is no God, Self-ownership and the Non-Aggression-Principle which might come from it is still not the sole valid way to organize society. This is because "valid" would, in the case of "no God", be without objective meaning. Those who think the smart should rule the dumb, the strong should rule the weak, or who have no preferences beyond their own needs, would in that case have philosophies which are as "just" as those based on Self-Ownership and the NAP. This is because absent a higher moral law (God is the lawgiver) there is no reference point for measuring "just."

The NAP then becomes just one possible framework for organizing a society of near-equals, so long as each individual thinks it is in their self-interest to do so. It is not the "right" answer for organization because there is no "right" answer, only answers which work in a given situation and those which don't.

In a Godless universe, if another group comes along, organized under other principles, a stronger group, and they decide to make the NAP group into laundry soap, then too bad. There is no transcendent moral basis for the NAP group to object to this action. The outsiders are not bound by your agreement. They are not bound to recognize it. Nor are the insiders bound by it, should circumstances change. No one is bound by anything. As Dostoyevsky penned in *The Brothers Karamazov*, "Without God....anything is permitted."

Again, I am not here to resolve the question of the existence of God. My point is that there is more than one set of beliefs around which to organize a government that are just as reasonable as Self-Ownership and the NAP, given their premises. And since we may never resolve whose premises are correct in this world, we should adopt a more live and let live approach toward philosophy of government. Ironically it is the anarchists who seem the most opposed to this concept!

Anarchist: *I can claim the right to self-ownership under the principle of homesteading. I was the first to claim ownership over myself after I came into existence.*

Localist: You can't out-first the First Cause.

I quote from Jeremiah 1:5, "Before I formed you in the womb I knew you; Before you were born I sanctified you; I ordained you a prophet to the nations."

Not a whole lot of "self-ownership" going on in that view. You may believe that view is incorrect, but others do not, and you can't disprove their premises. I can't, with certainty anyway, disprove an agnostic's premises. We cannot know scientifically which of us is correct so we have to do the best we can to walk in whatever light we think we have been given.

Anarchist: *"If you don't believe in "self-ownership" then your parents own you. However sovereign individuals cannot own one another or else they are depriving another of their right to Liberty."*

Localist: You are begging the question here. Your reasoning is a nice tight circle here because you assume a sovereign individual when this is tied up in the very point at issue.

Still, "Your parents own you" is a better answer than many have given. Ancestor worship is still around, I would argue though, that parents (of whom I am one) have a moral responsibility to act in the child's best interest, even while I assume a degree of control over their life that I could never justly do with a "sovereign" individual. I don't “own” my children. I am their *stewards* for a time, until they gain adulthood, just as I am the steward of my own life until I pass on. Of course I base that on my belief in a higher moral order established by God.

Anarchist: *So since your parents don't own you, and there are no gods; whom then owns you if not you? The state? I think not. The philosophy of Liberty hinges on the fact that no one has a higher claim to your life than you do.*

Localist: The Founder’s philosophy of liberty did not hinge on “the fact that no one has a higher claim to your life than you do.” The Founder’s philosophy of Liberty hinged on the fact that the One with the Highest Claim to all Creation granted man rights- rights that the state had no just business going beyond. We are supposed to be Free because the Creator made us Free. That is where the philosophy of Liberty comes from. We may not agree just exactly where those lines are that the state should not cross, but it has been a better world since the idea that those lines existed has gained traction.

If there is no God, only the material universe, then no one has "right of ownership" over you, not even you. This is because in such a case there are no "rights", just individual preferences with none more objectively correct than the other. "Ownership" would morally equal "possession" in such a case. It would not matter if it was obtained "justly" under the NAP or the Christian code, or "unjustly." Without a divine reference point it is all just personal preferences. Remember the quote “without God...all things are permitted.”

The NAP, absent a God, would just be an organizing principle that some might agree to as long as it was seen to be in the mutual self-interest of each member of a group. Should a stronger outside society exist, they could choose to capture the weaker NAP society and make its members into laundry soap with an equally valid moral claim- that is to say, none. This would not constitute a violation of "rights" because transcendent "rights" would not exist.

The language of "right" and "wrong" as universally applicable ideas is drawn from a view of existence which pre-supposes a single reference point for morality. Self-ownership conflicts with the idea of the NAP as a transcendent reference point for morality. If I own myself then I also can decide when and whether I wish to apply the NAP to my own life. If the NAP is some transcendent moral reference point to which I am obligated to be bound, then I *don't* own myself – which is of course the basis for the NAP as an organizing principle in the first place.

Anarchist: *We view you as the owner of yourself in the sense that you are in control of and responsible for your actions. Since you are responsible for your actions, you should bear the fruit of them and no other person has claim on those actions (for good or for naught) without your consent. You may view God as your owner, but he's not responsible for you forgetting to take the trash out last night.*

Localist: Right, I am responsible for how I deal with my garbage. But God has an opinion on it, and so would my neighbors if I decided to just scatter it about my property. The whole point is whether or not there is some Higher Standard which I can be held to by others, be they God or government acting in His stead. Where I live, I vote to be able to have the government fine my neighbors if they just scatter their garbage in the yard, rather than wait until the bacteria gets in my well to take them to court.

The bottom line is that the decision is not wholly yours when you live amongst others. You don't get unlimited discretion on how you deal with your own garbage until the flies actually spread the disease to your neighbor or what have you.

Here is the moral basis for what I would call "conservative" government: Society has a right to act preemptively to sanction a behavior based on what past generations have learned about what will cause someone else harm if continued. Society does not have to wait until one's reckless behavior actually results in harm. The recklessness itself is immoral and can be sanctioned because it shows a lack of regard for the potential to harm others. If we notice that methamphetamine use has caused a large percentage of people to go mad and violate the rights of others, we make the manufacture, sale and use of meth against the law. We do this despite an individual's objection that they have not lost control of their senses and hurt anyone yet.

We are not our own. We don't belong to the state either, or to our neighbors even, but each belongs to the Creator. What that means, we all have to hash out among ourselves until hopefully one day we approximate getting it right. The ultimate question here is whether or not each of us get a blank piece of paper to create a morality to suit us, or do we get that blank piece of paper only to draw, as best we can detect it, the moral order which exists out there independent of our wishes and opinions.

Challenges to the Practicality of God as a Source of Rights

"...the same revolutionary beliefs for which our forebears fought are still at issue around the globe--the belief that the rights of man come not from the generosity of the state but from the hand of God." – President John F. Kennedy, Inaugural address, Jan. 1961

As with the previous chapter, these statements are drawn from records of actual disputes with anarchists. They may seem like odd ideas to some readers, but I assure you that there are people out there who actually take similar positions, for the dialogue below is based on challenges from real people.

Anarchist: *Rights don't come from gods. If they did, then how come they can be taken from and taken back by men? Rights are won on the battlefield. Period. I don't recall any accounts of Jesus killing Redcoats.*

Your position is based on ideas which aren't true. You very much can have rights without the help of divine monarchy. Natural Rights, just like every other philosophical concept both good and bad, are products of the human mind. Some concepts, like natural rights, are born of reason and others like your silly cosmic King come from fear and ignorance of those who cannot handle that we don't have all the answers, and who must invent superstitious nonsense to explain the world around them.

You can force your religion on me by force, yes, but you would have to be a tyrant to do it. Because of that, you would be acting illegally by our standard of natural law. We would be justified in revolting and killing you and your theocracy by right of self-defense.

Even if there was a god or wizard or whatever nonsense you want to buy into; and it was assumed that natural law was some high level spell that only he could cast on humans, then self-ownership would still be the law since in order to force atheists to subscribe to the concept, the principle of the law would immediately be broken. Self-ownership is the highest provable claim on an individual which does not require the initiation of illegal force to secure.

The philosophy of liberty and the three pillars which define it will cease to exist when all of us who believe in them are dead and all written records are gone. They will return only when someone thinks them up again. This philosophy will only become "rights" when enough collectivists who oppose them are dead or defeated politically so that there is no one left who can block them. Your god has no part to play in it save to be a mental opiate used to keep up the morale of those who require it.

Localist: Nonsense? But We Agree!

You and I are actually saying the same thing in the case of there being no God. That is to say, that "rights" are relative in that case, not absolute. Some writer once pointed out, and it is a fascinating concept, that if we had evolved as herd animals or solo predators we might have a different morality and a different concept of "rights". And if your belief that there is no God is correct, and our view of morality and rights is solely a product of human mind and experience, then what our "rights" are would change as human thinking changed.

It is my view that this approach to "rights" is a dangerous slippery slope. I would rather have "X" amount of freedom granted by a Creator than "2X" amount granted by other humans- because humans are very changeable. A Creator, well by now He is what He is, eh?

Really I think if you will look at my language in the case of no Creator I am describing relative rights and so are you. I am just bluntly emphasizing the logical consequences of that assumption.

Now I need not remind you that the Founders took my view of Rights, or rather I took theirs, that they were the Gift of God. So I am on the side of some really smart people who advanced human freedom a considerable distance.

I also think that Jesus killed more redcoats than there were redcoats, all without hurting a soul. What He did was turn those tyrants into servants of the people by changing their hearts. He introduced a revolutionary new concept to government- that the ruler is the servant of all.

Matthew 20:25 (King James Version) says "You know that the rulers of the Gentiles lord it over them, and those who are great exercise authority over them. 26 Yet it shall not be so among you; but whoever desires to become great among you, let him be your servant. 27 And whoever desires to be first among you, let him be your slave."

It is no accident that the ideas of human rights and liberty sprang forth from those very nations whose heritage was protestant Christianity. It was no co-incidence, rather, there was something in the message of Christ that, when taken seriously, inevitably produced more human liberty.

Anarchist: *But even if there is a god, and even if he's the fellow who invented rights, so what? You say rights come to us by god. Big deal, they are taken from us by men. Seeing as men have the power to dominate and destroy those human rights that your god invented, what does it matter who invented them? When they are gone, they are gone. That means god given rights are every bit as arbitrary and fleeing as those dreamed up by human reason. No matter their origin, they must be won on the battlefield and kept through vigilant defense by us.*

I don't see how the origin, be it magical fairy-tale creatures or the human mind makes any difference whatsoever. I would however point out that you wouldn't be the first person on earth to assert that your particular belief system is sanctioned by a god. At least I know that what I believe is just that... a belief that is fragile and can be taken if not defended. I hold no illusions that magic beings with super-powers are going to defend my rights.

I would argue only that there is no provable claim of ownership of a human's life greater than his own. Therefore, whether you believe in god or do not, if you wish to have law based on free choice rather than coercion, gods cannot be the highest claim to our lives legally. You can submit your own ownership claim to your magic king, but you cannot submit mine without force which I would rebel against. This is why "self" ownership is one of the three pillars of individualism. Without it, the boat don't float.

Localist: It is true that rights "can be taken by men..." This does not mean that men can do so without offending the moral order of the universe in a way that has real-life consequences.

If something is in harmony with the higher moral order of the universe established by the Creator, it is never gone. The recognition of those rights from the state may be gone, but the state cannot change God's established order. The denial of due rights sets in motion forces which, absent any other factors, will itself correct the error. The brilliant William Penn once said that there has never been for any great length of time a good people with bad rulers or a bad people with good rulers.

Violations of rights by one set of rulers sets in motion forces which will lead to their overthrow and replacement by others. That is the good of the moral order. It acts like gravity to slowly pull down at tyranny and only with great effort on the part of the tyrant's minions is it maintained for long. And it has also been seen that one who appeals to this moral order has an ally, even in the hearts of their enemies.

If you are not presently rebelling against the capricious rule we have presently then I don't see what would induce you to do so under the much greater degree of freedom you would have in a Localist society. You may hold no "illusions" that magic beings will defend your rights, but if there are no divine beings, the illusion is that you have any "rights" at all. What you have then are "deal-killer" negotiating positions, not rights. That is, "this is the amount of my life that I will accept the public having a say in, anything beyond this and I will violently resist society's claim." The very word "right" is infused with moral pretense. It is the opposite of "wrong."

Delegation and Symmetry as Anarchist Arguments Against Localism

Localism is compatible with much libertarian thought, so long as it is not enforced via the central government, because it is just a framework to protect local autonomy. Instead of government devolving into one big box containing one set of rules, there are many little boxes which are protected from being swallowed up into the one big box. But what people put into those boxes is up to them.

One state could be libertarian, another limited-government conservative, and another, for however long the free market of government would permit it, could even be liberal. In that sense, Localism could be useful to minarchists who could accomplish in little steps what they could not achieve all at once- the actual implementation of their ideas.

Anarchist philosophy is more absolutist, and is only with great difficulty incorporated into any other framework. The logic of anarchist thought is sound, but I do take issue with some of the premises, and of course reasoning from faulty premises will lead to the wrong conclusion even if the logic is sound.

Delegation and Symmetry

I have already described my issues with "self-ownership" as understood by anarchists. Why do we own our paycheck? Well, we worked for it, we created the wealth it represents, we chose to provide a service, etc. I can't help but notice that none of these things apply to self-ownership. The reasons that we might give to say we own things don't apply to ourselves. But please read the chapter on that one again if you wish and let me move on to a related subject- the concepts of Ethical Symmetry and Delegation of Powers.

Ethical symmetry is the concept that what is moral for one man is moral for another. If one man claims rights or privileges that another man does not have, then we have ethical asymmetry. Anarchists attempt to apply this principle to make the case that government agents should not have any powers that an individual does not have, since any power a government has (according to this view) are powers delegated from other people.

That brings us to the related concept of delegation of powers. Under this view the government of the people cannot logically have powers or rights not delegated to it by the people. If I do not have the right to steal, nor does the government via its IRS agency. Someone must have the right to "steal" via taxation for the government to have that power. Therefore they claim mandatory taxation is immoral.

This view presupposes that government is wholly an institution of man. In our culture, this view is assumed to be true without contemplation, or even awareness that this is not the only possibility. Though this view is now thoughtlessly accepted as true, it was not the predominant view of the Western world for the last fifteen centuries prior to the 20th century. The view prior to that time was that expressed in the thirteenth chapter of the book of Romans. This is that government is an institution of God, intended to benefit man by serving as God's minister for certain limited functions.

In most of Western Europe, cabinet members are still given the title of “Minister” as an artifact of the past dominance of this view of man and state. In the American experiment a distaste for institutional state religion led to our government using the term “Secretary”, as in “Secretary of State” where Europe might use the title “Foreign Minister”, but the separation of any particular religious establishment (denomination) from the central government did not mean that this view of human government as a ministry of God was no longer accepted as true.

It was the entanglement of specific religious institutions with the state which was rejected, not the idea that government officials were acting, according to the dictates of their conscience, as ministers of God. Many state constitutions actually banned atheists from holding public office, and some still do (including the state where I am now typing these words), though such prohibitions are no longer enforced.

I know that the claims in the above few paragraphs might seem incredible to a reader in the present day, especially one whose mind has not been trained to think outside of their own culture and time. It is shocking how far and how fast things can change, so that the new generation loses knowledge which was once commonly held. How can it be that a specific view of government held to be true by the majority a bare two hundred years before now be so obscure that it is not even considered as a possibility by the typical citizen?

Much of the blame can be laid at the feet of our education system. America, and much of the west, moved away from a classical education which was designed to transfer a core body of knowledge from one generation to the next in favor of a modernist technological view of education which focused on learning specific skills and current events. A ruling class which increasingly rejected God personally were unlikely to favor the educational propagation of the concept that rulers were not the final authority, but merely servants and ministers accountable to God. They were much more taken with the idea that *they* were the final authority, and that God either did not exist or was irrelevant to government. And so it came to pass that the view of government held by our Founders and their forebears was at first de-emphasized, then ignored, and finally suppressed and denounced.

I understand that many readers have been conditioned to accept the idea that even if God exists, His existence is irrelevant to the subject of government. This is yet another example of an intellectually indefensible yet widely held view. Few things seem as irrational as the position that God exists yet He has nothing at all to say about that institution which now touches, indeed dominates, so many aspects of human existence.

I will have a bit more to say about how we came to be in this place in a bit, and I ask the reader who takes offense at my position to bear with me for a while longer and I will shortly explain myself, or rather how I think we got from there to here. First though, let me return to the subject at hand- delegation and symmetry as limits on government. The argument for symmetry and delegation as the only basis for a just government disappears once the assumptions upon which it rests are revealed as just one possible premise. What if the relationship between citizen and government is not symmetrical?

What I am getting at is that if there is a transcendent moral order, it "owns" us in the sense that it is our moral superior, not our equal. It owns the state too. That is to say, each individual does not get to re-create moral reality for his or her self from a blank sheet of paper. Nor does the state get to do so. Both the individual and the state start with a blank sheet of paper, but the moral order of the universe is what they are obligated to try and write out on that blank sheet of paper, though we all do so imperfectly. The state is not supreme over the individual, nor is the individual supreme over the state, both are fallible and neither are sovereign in a transcendent sense of the word. Both should be subject to the moral law.

But if there is a Creator (and the Founders believed there was, and He was the source of all rights) then, while we have freedom of choice in this life as to whether we care to recognize their sovereignty, the Creator would still be sovereign. The Creator would still be Sovereign on the same basis that we claim ownership of something we create. A Creator-Created relationship does not need to be symmetric in order to be just.

Nor would the "delegation" of powers be limited to actions one could justly take as an individual. The "delegation" comes from the Creator to the government, and from the Creator to the individual. The individual may delegate powers to their government, but they are not solely the individual's powers. They are recognizing a power beyond them, and giving their consent to the state to wield those powers.

The Declaration of Independence mentions that governments derive their just powers "from the consent of the governed." The consent of the governed is not equal to the "delegation of powers of the governed". There may be overlap, but that is not equivalence. Giving consent to a government to be governed in this context is recognition by a citizen that the government is acting as God's minister to, for example, restrain evil by protecting God-given rights.

Please note that this view of things does not rule out a minarchist state ordered around the non-aggression principle. One may be like Ron Paul and believe that the Creator's moral code is to grant the individual the maximum liberty possible without hurting others. Notice though, that the basis for such a view would not be individual sovereignty, rather it would be based on the NAP being a key component of the moral code. This is to say, the Sovereign gave the individual freedom to choose whether to conform to the moral code, not that the individual is the Sovereign over it.

The classic Christian position, which helped birth the governments which provided the most liberty in human history, did not share the premise that government is in a symmetrical relationship with its subjects, nor that its powers were limited to those of its subjects. The book of Romans in chapter thirteen describes agents of the state as "God's ministers" who are authorized to "honor those who do good and bring wrath on evil doers."

That does not sound like a symmetrical relationship to me! Nor does it sound like the powers of government are limited to a delegation of whatever powers an individual can have, at least on a morally relativistic basis. God can do things to us that we can't justly do to Him, because He created us and knows more than us and is purer than we are. He is the parent, we are the child: another well-known asymmetric relationship. An agent of the state then is acting on behalf of God to uphold His standards for civil government, whatever they may be.

Before one jumps up to condemn me for trying to "impose my morality" or being a “statist” or “authoritarian”, I should like to point out that the Non-Aggression Principle itself, when used as a law, is also an attempt to impose a specific morality. It says the lines should be here, and not there. Therefore if one wants the Non-Aggression principle as the sole basis for human government, then they are the ones trying to impose their morality more than I. I have coined the term "liberauthoritarians" to describe this group.

The definition of a "liberauthoritarian" is a libertarian who is so sure that their premises are the only possible valid ones that they would, if they could, deny others the right to form a government on any other basis.

To me, an attempt to build a government so that everyone must view the world alike is collectivist. An attempt to flip the narrative so that a localist is somehow the collectivist, or the statist, or the one imposing their own morality, is brazen hypocrisy. I am the one who wants government decentralized so that people can choose for themselves what the organizing principle of their government ought to be.

Advocates of the NAP are the ones seeking to impose a universal standard on all mankind. My concern is primarily with the locality in which I live. If people living elsewhere wish to do things differently, as long as they are there of their own choice, it's really not my business. Rules for the overall structure in a localist society would only be to insure that power is not consolidated and local self-determination could continue.

Of course, everyone who wishes to impose a universal standard on human behavior says that the code they attempt to impose on all is the most reasonable. Yet we find that "reasonable" conclusions can vary based on the starting premises. Localism allows for people with varying premises to all get their way where they live. Because of that, it is more "tolerant" than any conception of government, including those organized around the NAP.

I am not even saying that the Non-Aggression Principle is wrong. I can't know that. Maybe the Non-Aggression Principle is also the moral principle that the Divine Moral Order wants governments to operate under. Maybe a government set up with the Non-aggression principle as the law would produce the best government the world has ever seen. I am all for its adherents getting a chance to try it, and under localism they can. My personal belief is that the Non-Aggression Principle is just that, a principle. That is, something that is generally true, but to which there are exceptions. This varies from the definition of a law, which is something that is always true without exception.

What I reject is the premise on which "Ethical Symmetry" is based as applied to government. I don't share the premise that God does not exist. And I find it irrational to believe that He does exist, but that He has nothing to say about this most vital of human institutions which permeates so much of our lives. And if He does exist, and He does have ideas about what human government should be like, then those ideas would trump “ethical symmetry” as an organizing principle for government. There is no ethical symmetry between Creator and created.

Governments based on whatever ideas God had about where government should and should not operate would be more in harmony with the moral order than governments which determined where those lines were based on “ethical symmetry.” An exception of course, would be if God's ideas for human government gave “ethical symmetry” a prominent role. That single exception is certainly one possibility, it is just not the one outlined in scripture nor most rooted in the liberty tradition of the West.

Let me be clear though. I don't want a state church. I don't want an external theocracy (I do want one internal to each person). Obviously I am not a “Christian Dominionist” or else I would not favor a form of government which lets people figure the rules out for themselves. But you don't have to have any of that to believe that there is a moral order in the universe greater than mankind, and that to some extent mankind is better off if we seek to be shaped by it rather than trying to force the moral order to accommodate us.

Again, "Ethical Symmetry" is organizing government around the principle of "if you can't as an individual justly initiate force against me for something, then you can't delegate the government to do it either." They reason from the premise that government is only a human institution. If that premise is true then it makes sense that we can't delegate powers to government that we don't have. But once you reject the idea that God is irrelevant to government, that government is all about man, it then becomes reasonable to reject "Ethical Symmetry" as an organizing principle for human government.

When one is acting on behalf of another who is greater than they are, then they *can* justly behave in ways that they could not if they acting on their own authority. If I am a middle manager for a company, I can't go outside my department and start giving order to the department of another middle-manager and take over their department. But if the owner of the company authorizes me to do so, then I justly can.

Christians are told in scripture "do not take your own revenge." We are told that God will repay. We are also told that the State is His Minister to bring wrath on evil doers. The state is acting *with* the consent of the governed, but *as* (when it acts within moral reality) the minister of God. In other words, this is an asymmetric relationship where the state can justly do things to an individual that another individual cannot justly do.

I have a similar objection to Delegation as used by anarchists. The classical western view of this question is that God raises up governments, and when they grow either too just for their population or not just enough relative to their population, He brings them down. The individual, when they elect, set up, consent to, or recognize a government, are agreeing that this is the body they will accept as executing God's will with the respect to the establishment of justice.

This view of government has been lost, but it is consistent with the ideals on which much government in the West was founded. The quote which begins the next chapter from a man named Jonathan Mayhew, the Congregationalist Minister of Boston West Church just before the American Revolution, was typical of those who held this view of government. It is a perspective which has produced a lot of human liberty, and I believe could have produced even more if it had been sustained. Now whether that produces a government that is libertarian, classically liberal, or limited-government conservative or whatever is a different story, or likely one-hundred different stories depending on the character and desires of the people.

The main thing I want people to take away from this is that there is more than one possible right answer to some very fundamental questions, depending on which premises are true. Because of that, whatever kind of government you want to have, I hope you will see the benefit of getting there through a localist framework.

The Divine Right of Government

"It is blasphemy to call tyrants and oppressors, God's ministers. They are more properly the messengers of Satan to buffet us. No rulers are properly God's ministers, but such as are just, ruling in the fear of God. When once magistrates act contrary to their office, and the end of their institution; when they rob and ruin the public, instead of being guardians of its peace and welfare; they immediately cease to be the ordinance and ministers of God; and no more deserve that glorious character than common pirates and highwaymen." - Jonathan Mayhew (1720 – 1766), Congregational minister at West Church in Boston

I have asked the reader for patience in considering a view of things which may be alien to them, but not from our Heritage. I should give some account for where the ideas I hold have come from. This then is, as briefly as I can give it, an explanation, an account of the evolution of thought about God and government in human history. It will necessarily be imprecise due to brevity, but this is the general gist of the subject:

From the time of the first central states in Babylon through the age of the Roman Empire, kings took upon themselves the mantle of the divine. In the first states there was no "separation between church and state", for the priests served the king. Religion was at the service of the state, and the rulers often presented themselves as descendants of the gods, if not gods themselves. The great mass of humanity existed to elevate the state, which was personified in the form of the King or Emperor.

The main exception to the rule was a collection of tribes in the Levant who for three hundred and sixty years elected their own local leaders, had a fixed law, a traveling judiciary, and no national executive at all except for brief periods of national emergency. When they finally decided to have a king, the priesthood was already long established, and for a time maintained its independence from the state. Over time this independence broke down, but so did the expression of the faith through a priesthood. Prophets rose up and they were the main movers and shakers of the faith, challenging both Kings and Priests.

In the Jewish tradition Kings were not gods whose will was law. There was a Higher Law, established by the One True God, and to that law both King and commoner were equally bound. Indeed King and Priest were to remain separate offices, only to be united in the person of Messiah, who alone was worthy to be both King and High Priest. The Messiah was the King of Kings, to whom all earthly Kings would be obligated to submit. Kings had a king- the King of Kings. They did not dictate the will of heaven to the masses, for kings were just as subject to it as they were.

As Christianity spread into Europe so did these ideas, for Christianity is not so much a separate religion from Judaism as it is Judaism fulfilled. Like all powerful people not used to, or happy with, restraints on their behavior, Kings attempted to use the parts of Christian scripture and tradition which were favorable to civil authorities to their best advantage. This took the form of the doctrine of the "Divine Right of Kings."

Passages of scripture such as the thirteenth chapter of the book of Romans and the second chapter of First Peter inform us that civil authorities exist by God's permission, and are sent as His Ministers. That is, they are in charge because God ordained it so.

The kings most favorable to this doctrine tended to forget that any divine *right* that kings had was balanced by divine *responsibilities* which kings had. Should a king fail to exercise their "rights" responsibly, their subjects reasoned, then the king himself was in rebellion against the Divine order. The quote cited at the beginning of this chapter was an example of such thinking.

After all, didn't the same passages of scripture which taught that rulers were established by God also teach that those rulers, wittingly or unwittingly, were Ministers of God? And didn't the same passage (Romans 13) describe this ministry as "honoring those who do *good*" and "bringing wrath on *evil* doers"? What if a ruler failed to do this? What if they did the opposite of this?

It was thinking along this line, starting from the basis that religion was above the state and not a function of state, which established what we know today as "the right of rebellion". From this it was deduced that a just government required "the consent of the governed" to its claim of a divine mandate. The people being governed had to agree that those doing the governing were doing so in a legitimate manner.

Notice that even the doctrine of the "Divine Right of Kings", one-sided though it was, was less totalitarian than the old pagan view. The old pagan view was that the state was the dignitary of the gods on earth and that the will of the king was the will of heaven. In contrast, Kings who had a Divine Right to rule *can* be in error and offend the Divine. Kings which are divine themselves cannot; their word is absolute, they are accountable only to themselves. When heaven and king are separated, then certain things were rightly beyond the reach of even the King. Not so when King and the will of Heaven are viewed as one and the same.

From this idea of separation of King from the Divine it was but a short leap to the idea that the common people could be their own kings as it were, sharing power in a Republican form of government. The Creator was still viewed as the source of rights (as noted for example in the Declaration of Independence), but He didn't just give the governing authorities a Divine Legitimacy to govern. He also gave individual persons legitimate claims against governments which exceeded their Divine mandate.

In other words, individuals had rights. The idea that there lives a King of Kings translated into the idea that there were just limits on the power of the state. The earthly King or ruler was not the Master of the people rather they were ministers acting on behalf of God, the true Master of both King and Commoner. This idea held even in a nation where the People themselves were the king.

The same God which gave rulers the authority to rule also placed boundaries on that authority for the sake of the individual, which was actually the point of government. Not like the Pharaohs, who considered the purpose of his subject's lives was to glorify the state and his own royal person by slaving away at constructing elaborate tombs. Rather, government existed for the purpose of upholding justice. Glorification of the state was not the purpose of the citizen's lives, or the reason for government. Rather the state existed to *serve* the individual by providing justice.

As it is recorded in scripture (Luke 22 *et al*), in the Kingdom of Heaven to "rule" is to "serve". This view of government was a wellspring of human liberty. It was the basis on which the Democracies and Republics of the West were established.

For much of this period most education was conducted by the church or by local communities. It is not surprising then that during that time educated persons were trained to understand that the state was not absolute, that even the king (or Parliament) is but a minister of God and is duty-bound to rule justly, and that individuals could claim rights even against the mighty state. This policy carried over into America, where the people as a whole were supposed to rule. That is, a Bill of Rights was recognized which constituted areas of life beyond the just reach of the government and therefore not subject to majority vote.

As the central state itself began to take over education this doctrine limiting government was at first de-emphasized, then ignored, and now suppressed. In its place the post-modern state is not devising a new system, but re-incarnating an old one. A neo-pagan view of government is now emerging which claims that there is no Divine Will separate from and above the state, or if there is it is mandatory that the state disregard it. I fear it will end in a Collective Man imagining ourselves as the new god, and some new Caesar claiming to speak for “the people" will represent this "god's" will on earth.

The current crop of "progressives" is not bringing humankind progress at all, but rather regression to an oppressive period of human history where the desires of the state triumphed over the will of the individual without limitation. In Roman times the Emperors made themselves out to be gods and used the state as their instruments to enforce their "divine" whim.

In the new order a vast collective called "The People" will insert itself into the role of the Divine, using the state to enforce its whims. The voice of the people will be considered the voice of God. In this view "rights" can only be mere grants of the state, not something the individual is entitled to by a Power above it. "Rights" are thereby transformed from *restrictions* on the state to political tools *of* the state. They become the means by which groups favored by the state are granted new privileges at the expense of the disfavored group's freedom.

At that point the substance of individual rights, as claims by individuals against the state, will vanish. The language of "rights" may persist without substance for some time, but only to be used by whatever small group is really running things as a fig-leaf to cover the state's trampling over some groups in favor of others.

Our only hope of sustaining liberty is for us to revert to the view of government which produced it. If the idea that government was accountable to God restrained the state under the old view, what now restrains it under the new view that the existence of God is irrelevant to government? The end of this will not be a government without god, but rather the false god of humanity collectively deifying itself under a new "divine" ruler. A government which claims no need of a divine right to govern will acknowledge no divine limitations on its governance.

"And can the liberties of a nation be thought secure when we have removed their only firm basis, a conviction in the minds of the people that these liberties are the gift of God? That they are not to be violated but with his wrath?"

- Thomas Jefferson, Notes on the State of Virginia Query #18, 1781

Individual Rights vs. the Collective

"Man is not free unless government is limited."

– Ronald Reagan

Some anarchists have accused Localists of being collectivists, so long as the collectivism is done at the local level rather than the national level. That is, that localists think rights don't exist unless granted by the locality. This charge is untrue, though unsurprising. Anarchists are fond of calling everyone else "collectivists", or perhaps "statists"- even minarchist Libertarians.

Localism, a Philosophy of Government explicitly stated in the chapter on "The First Pillar of Localism" that individual rights exist whether or not any government wishes to acknowledge them. Localism is meant to be exercised under a Republican form of government. By definition, a Republic is a government organized around an agreement that government power will be limited; that individuals have certain claims against the state which are not subject to majority vote. Rather, there are limits on what the state can do or not do to the individual regardless of whether or not the majority wish it.

These limits are typically spelled out in a compact or constitution which establishes the government and which cannot be changed except by extra-ordinary measures. The Bill of Rights is an example of a list of things which are supposed to be "off-limits" to the federal government and not subject to majority vote. Even if Congress, in accordance with the will of most of their constituents, wants to interfere in freedom of speech, freedom of religion, etc, they are bound by the compact against it (making sure they *stay* bound by what's in that compact was sort of the point of *Localism, a Philosophy of Government*).

The list of rights does not have to be inclusive. For example, the last amendment to the Bill of Rights basically said that "We can also have rights not on this list. Just because we can't think of anything else right now does not mean that we can't think of some more we will want to claim in the future, and we reserve the power to do so."

Libertarian thought, of the minarchist variety at least, takes the idea of a Republic to its limit. Instead of providing a list, even an open-ended list, of recognized individual rights wherein government may not legislate, it produces a short list of areas where government is *permitted* to legislate, declaring all the rest of life off-limits to government intervention. One can easily see that minarchist libertarianism is simply the far end of the same spectrum on which we can find the limited-government conservative or classical liberal, constitutionalist, etc... As the list of recognized rights gets longer and longer, the government begins to look more and more like a minarchist state.

What makes individualists different from collectivists is that individualists believe that there are areas of life which ought to be off-limits to government and thus not subject to a vote of the majority. A collectivist acknowledges no such limits. Not only is dissent from the collective viewed as illegitimate, but it is almost viewed as a disease or a threat to the whole.

To the collectivist, there is no question which is not subject to public approval, and no area of life which is outside the just control of the state. Whatever you think you own is owned only with the approval of the whole, and whatever you do is done only by the approval of the whole. Everything is subject to the will of "the People" as a collective entity.

Individualists of all stripes reject this diabolical philosophy and are united in the belief that there are large areas of life which ought to be off limits to government. Where they may not agree is exactly how much leeway on personal behavior is reserved to the individual and how much of life is justly subject to public approval. The line where true rights end and public interests begin is subject to various opinions, but there is no doubt among individualists of all stripes that, as Ronald Reagan once said "man is not free unless government is limited."

This is also the position of the localist. I believe it is the same position the Founders had, that we are endowed by our Creator with rights. These pre-exist the state and don't depend on recognition from the state to be legitimate. I believe that the state cannot violate those rights without committing injustice.

This does not mean that each individual gets to determine for themselves what their rights are and this somehow obligates others to respect their opinion. Sure each citizen can have their own view on what rights their Creator granted us, but our neighbors are not obliged to accept our views. That's a good thing too. Man recognizes rights, he does not give them, lest what we as men grant to ourselves is taken away with the same authority, that of mere men, with which it was given.

What this boiled down to in the American Experiment is that the Founders drew up a list of rights, a Bill of Rights plus some other restrictions on the state in the constitution. It amounted to saying "here is how much individual freedom we trust giving each other. Here are things we know should be taken out from under the purview of government, and not subject to a majority vote."

Thus while it may be so that no government is obligated by what *we* think our rights are, in a Republic a government *is* obligated by the compact which formed it to respect what *that compact* says that our rights are. This fundamental idea is known as "the rule of law". The government should obey its own rules and the limits under which it was established. It is the one pillar of libertarian thought with which I am in full agreement!

The application of the rights which we legitimately have is another potential gray area. While we do have rights, in interactions with others we are not always the best judges of how our own rights are applied. We are not objective in how we apply our own rights. Therefore we have civil authorities which are supposed to apply the law and apply the rights impartially. Those authorities are definitely not always objective either, and that is why they themselves must be subjected to something- not only the checks and balances of a Republic, but also the free market as described in *Localism, A Philosophy of Government.*

So we see there is an ongoing tension between what any given individual thinks that their rights ought to be, what their rights really are by the absolute moral order of the universe established by the Creator, and the list of recognized rights by the government. The more those three are in harmony, the most just and peaceful the society.

While various forms of individualists will have disagreements about what should be on this list and what should not be, unlike collectivists, they believe in the limitations. They believe there is a list of areas of life which are rightly left to the individual and not subject to majority vote or government approval. They may have different ideas about what ought to be on that list, but they believe that list is not just a matter of personal preference, but of transcendent justice and morality. Call, it if you will "Heaven's List of Rights" that the Creator has granted to the individual, which no government can violate without committing an injustice.

Heaven's List of Rights

I use the term "Heaven's List of Rights" to describe all of the individual rights which the Creator, who in the view of the Founders gave us our rights, wants people to have. What should be on the list? What should be off the list? I have heard many suggestions over the years and my confidence in anyone's answers is almost inversely proportional to the confidence they have in those answers.

What exactly are our God given rights, and how are they to be applied? Not even the Founders knew for certain. They made their list of things that they all agreed were God-give rights, then they added for safe measure the tenth amendment which said that the list was not all inclusive. The tenth amendment said that the states and the people could still in the future claim rights against the central government which were not on the list!

On the other hand, it is also clear that even the rights that were expressly listed and the limitations on government which were plainly spelled out presupposed that the population had virtue enough to use such freedom judiciously. In 1798 the father of the Constitution, James Madison, wrote these words to the men of the Massachusetts Militia: "Our Constitution was made only for a moral and religious people.

It is wholly inadequate to the government of any other." He wrote in that same letter that human moral failures could rip the cords of the Constitution "like a whale goes through a net."

Clearly, Madison was of the view that whatever the theoretical maximum amount of rights people could have, the *operational* maximum was dependent on maintaining a certain level of virtue in the populace. Should our behavior fall below a certain threshold of decency, never mind what additional rights we think we might be entitled to, we will not even be able to sustain the ones which we have inherited!

It seems to me that the more virtuous the population, the larger the proportion of their total potential maximum rights must be recognized by the state. Virtuous people, in the traditional sense of the word, just don't need much government. If indeed government is there to "honor those who do good and bring wrath on evil doers" what use is it among people who do good without the need for kudos and are disinclined to do evil? For such a people external government becomes more and more a useless, bothersome, and expensive relic.

It is little wonder then that many government programs serve to undermine the morality of the public. By encouraging immorality, those who rule create an environment where there is more need for their "services." A virtuous population is the best defense against big government, for such people have no need of masters.

So what is on "Heaven's List of Rights"? I submit to you that the answer depends on from where one is asking the question. Heaven is unchanging in its basic attributes of goodness. In Heaven, a place of maximum virtue, the population may be safely granted maximum personal freedom. This makes the pertinent question for us "What is Heaven's List of Rights *for us* as a people? Given where we are, how much freedom and lack of external constraint can we safely handle?"

Insofar as this earth goes I suggest to you that there is no one list of rights, nor only one right way to apply them for all populations at all times. Rather, "Heaven's List of Rights" on earth is a dynamic relationship between the virtue of a population and the amount of freedom which they may possess without an increase in injustice. The "just" amount of freedom which any people ought to have depends in part on how virtuous they themselves might be. The just may safely be granted more freedom than the unjust.

Let me attempt to explain that last proposition. I am not suggesting moral relativity, but a moral relationship. I am sure that you dear reader will agree that with freedom comes responsibility. Irresponsible people are short on virtue and don't stay free long. Thomas Jefferson noted "If a nation expects to be ignorant and free, in a state of civilization, it expects what never was and never will be." I suggest that many populations for much of history lacked the virtue required to sustain self-government with the extensive individual rights as our fore-fathers knew them. It therefore mattered less if their governments did not respect their rights.

What I mean is, a lawless people would only use freedom to destroy themselves and trouble their neighbors, resulting in chaos. Because of that, immoral governments which did not respect the rights of the people still had "legitimacy" in such a population. That is to say, they still had value in restraining evil because as bad as they were, without them violence and the violation of rights from private threats would be worse. In short, when people do not respect one another's rights then it enables and legitimizes a government which does not respect them either.

Each of us can probably think of situations from recent history where a nation has had a strongman or tyrant deposed and instead of things getting better, things got worse. Instead of the strongman stepping on necks, the people used their new found freedom to step on each other's necks. Private violations of rights increased more than public violations of rights decreased, and there was more injustice than before.

With the rise of Christianity in the West, populations attained a level of virtue such that they did not *need* to be governed so much. The people were largely capable of self-rule. When people respect each other's rights then the violations of rights coming from the rulers becomes much more glaring. In a nation of relative angels, an abundance of rules and codes and penalties and government becomes just so much needless overhead (at best). It is only found useful when people fear what their neighbors might do.

What we can say then is that if men were angels, we could expand "rights", that is, things not subject to majority vote, infinitely. Since men are not angels, if we expand rights (areas of life which are not subject to government) beyond the virtue of the population, then lawlessness can multiply. Injustice is free to occur without the restraint of law in whatever area of life we have ceded to the individual.

So how do we find "the right answer" with respect to what rights ought to be recognized by our government? Even if there may be only one "Heaven's List" of Creator-granted rights, no one knows the totality of that list. Plus, given the variables involved, there can still be more than one "right" answer to the question.

For example, say there were no laws against drug use, even addictive drug use, and no speed limit laws or laws against driving while intoxicated. No one is prosecuted until actual harm is done to another. That would represent an increase in freedom, but if that freedom was not used responsibly by the entire population then it would be easy to suppose that more harm would be done to others than there would be if state sanctions against these things were in place.

The exception would be in a population so virtuous that none of them would use drugs or alcohol irresponsibly, or drive at unsafe speeds. In that case the laws would just represent an extra expense and loss of freedom. But with a population of men, not angels, some harm would be averted by the loss of freedom. Further, the more irresponsible the population, the more harm would be averted by making these things subject to state prohibition. Thus there is a dynamic relationship

The relationship might be expressed as a formula. The goal is to protect people's rights, from both public threats and private threats, to the maximum extent possible. Let's take population "A", with a level of virtue at point "Y", and say that granting the whole list of "rights" (100%) on Heaven's list might give them the freedom to do "X" amount of harm and injustice to one another via private threats to individual rights.

What sort of things constitute "X" amount? An example might be a person with few personal assets and low capacity to earn income getting high on drugs and driving at 100 miles per hour until they run over and kill two children. Laws against speeding, or certain drug use, or driving while intoxicated, would lower the incidence of such painful events, but the enforcement of such laws comes at a price even to those who never drive irresponsibly.

Giving people 100% freedom from government regulation in our scenario above resulted in "X" amount of harm and violations of rights from private threats. So let's suppose we come in and reduce 100% freedom from government regulation to

50% freedom from government regulation (100%/2) in order to prevent such occurrences.

So then "50% freedom from government regulation" represents a state which regulates half of our lives rather than none of it. Further, assume as a result of this that there were random traffic stops, an expensive enforcement apparatus which must be paid for with coercive taxes, and mandatory drug tests and the like. Public Threats to liberty then becomes a factor. People have been wrongly killed at police stops too.

It is easy to see that the state could get so carried away with "safety" that they could wind up by degrees costing people just as much (or more) liberty than the occasional drug-addled driver. If just as much, then the total amount of injustice and violation of rights is still "X".

So we had "X" amount of injustice from private threats to rights when there was little or no state, and we still had "X" amount of injustice when the state regulates 50% of our lives, it just came through a combination of public and private threats.

The population suffers the same amount of injustice ("X") one way or the other, so for the purposes of establishing justice, setting the bar at either 100% or 100%/2 results in equally desirable outcomes regarding the amount of injustice.

That outcome is with the virtue of the population at point "Y". Were the population any worse (Y-1), it would be preferable to set the "rights bar" at 100%/2. That is to say, if the population were less virtuous than they were, there would be less injustice having the state regulate 50% of their life than none of their life.

If on the other hand the population were any more virtuous (Y+1), then a figure closer to 100% freedom from government would produce a more just result. The more virtuous the population, the more freedom they can enjoy.

What then is to be done in our government in our time? We have to poke around and try to find the best answer, what we see through a glass darkly. Various places can have somewhat different answers. Let each state try what they think, and each county modify it if they see fit, and then let's see what works. Let's see how much freedom people can have before it is clear we have moved beyond the list of heaven. Or perhaps I should say, beyond the amount of heaven people are ready to handle.

Will a society organized around the NAP be the best one? I don't think so, but if people are virtuous enough it could be. At any rate, people should have the power to try it, if they can get one another to agree to trust each other with that much latitude in their conduct.

Right now it is obvious to me that the central state in America is at least as big a threat to our rights as my fellow citizens are. My view is that this is mostly because it is not respecting the individual rights listed in the compact by which the central state was established. That is, this is a Rule of Law issue more than a "the list of rights should be longer" issue.

The present government is not just violating what I think ought to be my rights, they are violating what the compact by which they were formed (the Constitution) explicitly states are my rights. Even if they are not bound by my view of what my rights ought to be, they ought at least to be bound by the view of individual rights in the compact by which their authority to govern is granted!

The abuse of "rights" by the central state goes beyond that though. They are also creating fake group "rights" not stated in the compact, and using those invented "rights" for their chosen groups as a wedge to separate me and others like me from self-government., and even from how I use my own property or who I associate with.

You see, it is possible to go beyond "Heaven's List of Rights" in the other direction as well. The state has an obligation under this view of government to recognize our legitimate rights but it also has an obligation to not pervert this function into a means to separate people from self-government by abusing the language of rights. The state can transgress by adding to the list things which are not true rights at all. It can go beyond the mandate of Heaven to give collective pseudo-rights to favored groups at the expense of true personal liberty.

By way of example, imagine a government which decided group "A" had a "right" to the earnings and wealth of group "B". Such looting under the guise of "rights" would soon have the people of a nation forming coalitions to loot one another, resulting in a great loss of personal liberty for all. It is not always true that more listed "rights" is better. What is listed as a right must conform to the moral reality of the universe in order to really decrease injustice. It should not fall short of this standard, nor go beyond it.

The power to define "rights" is the power of dictatorship, since rights by definition are not subject to majority vote. That is why the first pillar of localism is that even the power to define rights must be decentralized. The central government of the United States presently offends in both directions. It acts outside of the rule of law by ignoring rights which are explicitly recognized in the compact by which it is authorized to govern. At the same time it manufactures specious new pseudo-rights which it uses to deny citizens self-government and erode personal liberty.

That's why we should work intelligently and diligently to decentralize that and every other power government has. We still need government, until we are angels, but we have to keep it localized or it quickly turns from servant to master. Localism not only recognizes that, but it sets up a framework to keep local power from falling prey to the ambitious centralizers.

If men were angels, indeed anarchism would work. There is no need at all for an external law in a place where the law of God is written on every heart. Whatever might be on "Heaven's List of rights" for us here on earth, that list is longer in Heaven itself. It can only be so in that one divine realm where men have been so refined that every wish of their innermost being can be made into reality at once without any fear of such power being used for ill.

I find it ironic that some Limited-Government Christian Conservatives rail at atheist anarchists who insist on the NAP as the do-all end-all, while the latter rail even more at the former for trying to violate their "rights." God's perfect will is surely that external government be as limited as possible, for that is how it appears it will be in His kingdom. The whole scope of scripture takes mankind from a place where the law is external, detailed, voluminous, and moves us to the place where the Creator offers to write His laws on the tablets of our hearts. That is, no external rules are needed. The Kingdom of Heaven, as Jesus stated, is not coming with signs to be observed. Instead, it is in the midst of those who need no law to compel them to do the right things.

God in His perfect will seems to be quite voluntaryist, but that same Divine will subjected the children of Israel to conquest and oppression when their personal behavior became such that their freedom was used to wrong Him and one another. They misused their freedom so badly, that He who is

Mercy decided that they would actually be better off, for a time, as slaves.

When Christ spoke out against serial marriage, his questioners asked why, if divorce was so bad, was there provision for it in the Law of Moses? Christ's answer (Matthew the nineteenth chapter) was that this provision was given because of their hardness of heart, it was not a reflection of God's ideal.

That might be the way we should look at most earthly laws, concessions to the impurities of the human condition rather than the ultimate Divine intent. He means for us to be free, wholly free, if only our hearts were in a place where such freedom would not lead us to dark outcomes.

To sum up, I will note that even in the Old Testament God seemed to have some localist leanings. Read First Samuel Chapter 8 and you will find that God is not a fan of a strong central executive. Ancient Israel was a proto-localist society, a decentralized state which lasted longer than America has lasted and failed for the same reason we will fail- a multi-generational loss of personal virtue in the population.

The conclusion is that what is on "Heaven's List of rights" as applied to us on earth is not so fixed as some might suppose, but ebbs and flows with the character of the people in a particular society. The better men serve The Master, the less need they have of human masters. The more lawful the people, the more freedom they must be given by their rulers in order to sustain the ruler's legitimacy.

Localism is not a system which says that rights come from the collective, be it a local collective or a central one. It is a system which says rights are God-given, but that our knowledge of them and how they are applied is not perfect. We lack certainty as to how the outer limits of these rights are applied in some situations. It also says that whatever rights we are sure of are better protected if there is competition among governments in protecting them rather than entrusting all the power to protect them to a single distant source.

We as individuals can't always be our own final judge of what are rights are and how they should be applied in a given situation, because we are the furthest thing from impartial judges on such matters. But at the least we can have a system which allows for a variety of answers, at the margin, to such questions. In this variety we have the best chance to live among those who see, and exercise, the administration of justice similar to the way we do.

Localism works within the framework of a Republic, in which a given set of rights has already been recognized in the compact which established the society. The majority is properly bound by what my rights are as stated in that compact. To be clear, the majority is not bound by my belief of what my rights *ought* to be, but is bound by what rights are stated in the language of the compact which established the state. Rights are those things which are properly left to the individual and not subject to majority vote. State respect for these limits is a part of the fundamental principle of justice called "The Rule of Law".

Answers on Defense Spending, Voluntary, Mandatory, or Decentralized?

I would now like to move from a philosophical discourse on rights to specific areas of government where the anarchist view is unworkable. One such area is spending for defense. Now, the most common rebuttal to complaints about anarchist "solutions" on national defense is that the central state's solutions on national defense are deeply flawed. That accusation is true, but it does not undo the difficulties with the anarchist view, it only highlights the need for a third solution which localism provides.

"The Free Rider Problem" is, whether admitted or not, problematic for advocates of the various factions of anarchism and voluntarism. They hold to a radical (they would say consistent) view of self-ownership and the Non-Aggression Principle as it pertains to taxation. They believe that all taxes should be voluntary, and that mandatory taxation is tyranny, since it violates both the Non-Aggression Principle and the Principle of Self-Ownership. The idea that no government on any level should have the power to coerce tax revenues means that any "taxes" paid in a voluntary society would be more like donations or personal purchases.

Of course many taxes in our day and time are unjust. They are legalized plunder of one subset of the population in order to bribe another subset of the population. This is true of much government spending in our time, but not all such spending. Some items are true “public use goods”. A public use good is one in which it is difficult to exclude people from obtaining the benefits of that good regardless of whether or not they have paid for it.

The difficulty with removing the power to collect coercive taxes for anything is that "public use" goods will be greatly under-consumed in a voluntary system. This will lead to not only a misallocation of resources, but in some cases a loss of the very freedom libertarians and others hold so dear.

National Defense is a prime example of a public good. You benefit from national defense (note: this argument applies to true national defense, not militarism masquerading as such) whether you contribute to the national defense or not. It would be impossible to exclude you from the benefits of national defense. Again, that's the profile of a "public use" good. You can obtain full benefits even if you did not contribute toward the purchase.

Suppose we achieve anarchy and the volunteer tax collector comes around and asks you how much you want to spend on defense this year. To reflect our real defense budget, excluding the wars in Iraq and Afghanistan, the share for the average family of four would be about $9,000 per year (you might not have known the burden was so high). The fellow tells you that to keep defense spending where it is, he needs you to write a check for $9,000, or actually $18,000 since your humble author decided things were a little tight in my household this year so I told them I didn't want to pay anything.

Who among you will honestly tell me that you will keep writing that check, year after year? How long will you do it knowing that it will just be one drop in a very big bucket? A bucket that won't even notice that "drop" of yours, which is such a sacrifice for you?

I have heard it said that giant corporations like Coca-Cola, with so much to lose, would step up and pay the bills. Please, corporations don't care which set of government parasites is looting them, only how much they loot. "Meet the new boss, same as the old boss" would be their motto. They may even negotiate a better deal for themselves with the “new boss”.

Jefferson was right, merchants have no country. Corporations may even look on the absorption of one nation by another as an opportunity to expand their markets. Besides, if corporations were paying the bills, they'd be calling the literal "shots" even more than they do now- sending our troops overseas to protect their foreign property as a condition of their continued support. Don't count on them to defend your freedom, because that is not what they are there for. They have their own interests.

In a voluntary society, if we just go around asking everyone how much they want to pay for national defense, the answer would be "X", even when a citizen really thought the prudent level would be 2X, or 10X or even more. Defense will be woefully under-consumed in a voluntary society. Dangerously so. It has been said that short of the Kingdom of God, those who beat their swords into plowshares will plow for those who don't.

A society which funds its national defense this way will lose its freedom to a society which does not. Any who doubt this please cite examples of any society of any size in the last thousand years which has long survived by so funding their national defense.

The American Revolution was not supported by the entire population, but the entire population was taxed to pay for it. Had we not done so, we would have lost. Could either side have won the First World War with such a system? How about the Second World War?

That's the problem with voluntarism and public goods such as police protection and national defense. Resources are not rationally allocated because we all know we can be a free rider when things are tight, and things tend to always be tight!

Some anarchists have proposed a private insurance model in lieu of a traditional military. By so doing they imagine they have gotten round the free-rider problem. Of course this is not so. If the rest of the citizens in your city are protected by State Farm's armor divisions from invasion then your home is also protected. You cannot be excluded from the benefits even if you are a free-rider.

Further, rather than insurance organically filling the needs in our present society, we find that the state must mandate the purchase of insurance in all circumstances where the individual might otherwise shift the cost to others. One example would be stiffing the bank if one's home burns down and one has no homeowner's insurance, another example would be not having automobile insurance which covers harm to other drivers. People act in their own self- interest, and that includes not buying any more insurance than they can get away with.

Counting on an insurance model for public defense is ludicrous on another level as well. Even though the government makes us buy insurance when we otherwise might not, it makes up for it to some extent by requiring insurance to pay off claims when they otherwise might not.

Insurance companies use every trick in the book to get out of paying claims. Sometimes they get shamed by a media story into paying (we hear of such horror stories on a regular basis), but at least as often they do pay because the government which gives them a license to peddle their product makes them pay. What reasonable expectation can we have that an insurance company in an anarchist society would wage a costly war to protect us when we can't presently count on them to pay their claims without a government around to make them? It is more likely that they would act in their own self-interest, which means that they would perform their part of the contract when it did not cost them much and then run ads bragging about it, while looking for some loophole to avoid their obligations when poorer clients faced more expensive troubles.

Even if somehow all the insurance companies wanted to perform as their clients expected, what evidence is there that such a model can actually do the job? I have an image in my mind of panzers rolling up to the outskirts of my city and I respond by placing a call to my portly insurance agent. What is he going to do?

Even if his agency has a team of mercenaries at the ready, mercenaries don't tend to fight as hard as the troops for nation states whose soldiers really believe in the cause of their flag. War is too difficult for the soldiers in the field to respond solely to the profit motive.

But of course, it is not fair to compare a voluntary society with perfection. Comparing it to what we have now would be a much fairer comparison, and in that comparison it looks a lot better. This is because what we have now is a massive over-consumption of goods- the opposite problem of the free-rider problem in public use goods.

That too is a result of the way defense is funded. The people paying for it are only distantly connected to those who decide how much to pay. And between them is a military-industrial complex which lobbies the people who decide how much we need. It lobbies them intensely. The Complex is focused on only one issue- how much money the defense industry is getting.

For the general voter, a Congressman who spends too much on defense can make up for it in other areas. But for the Military-Industrial Complex, there are no other areas. Breaking it down to incentives for politicians, they have more incentive to overspend defense dollars than under spend them.

If that were the only economic incentive, it could be overcome. After all, they would just be another special interest group in Washington with few boots on the ground back home. Two things have enabled this special interest to successfully get America to overspend on defense, or really just one thing that has two components. Defense is overconsumed in our society today because the cost for it is shifted to others.

One way this is done is through the use of fiat currency debt to fund the purchases. This allows the politicians to essentially buy the favor of the special interest while shifting the costs unto the backs of the unborn, who have no vote to defend themselves from such plundering. Taxing the next generation to buy support is a favorite tactic of politicians lacking in moral character. Since we don't have to write the check for it today, we choose to tackle more immediate problems. Meanwhile the debt bomb just keeps ticking.

The other way costs are shifted is that specific defense spending, which benefits specific localities where such systems are built, is paid for from general revenues. In other words, the politicians are taxing all the other states to pay for spending in their state. This is the old "if you are paying, I'll have the filet mignon" problem. When costs are shared evenly no matter how the benefits are divided, people tend to consume more than they would if they had to pay all of the costs themselves.

And of course, when you have all this excess military hanging around, there are a lot of interests that can find work for it- precipitating more "defense" spending on wars, bases, occupations, nation building, and "kinetic actions" which have more to do with protecting the foreign property of some global corporation than the actual country.

So while we could look down our long noses at voluntarism and castigate it for risking the freedom it claims to be protecting by under consuming defense spending, we'd better be careful. The way we are doing business now has just as big a problem- we are spending ourselves into debt slavery.

How can we find balance? If we place a mandatory tax on people for a public good, we set in motion forces which will tend to insure that defense spending is over-consumed, in particular once a specialized industry has grown up around it. If we make taxes voluntary for a public good, we virtually guarantee that it will be irrationally under-consumed, risking our freedom to those less scrupulous about how they fund their military. As usual, we seek for a balance between two unsound extremes, one of which is unfortunately our present condition.

I believe the approach presented in Localism represents the best possible answer in a very imperfect world. Neither the Voluntary answer on defense nor the Mandatory answer on defense adequately considers the unintended economic consequences of their policies. We need an integrated and considered approach which balances the extremes of these two methods in a way that will produce optimal allocation of resources and maximization of individual liberty. Localism provides this balance.

Yes, in Localism taxes are mandatory for public use goods, but due to the manner in which the philosophy decentralizes the military, money, debt, and corporations, the perverse incentives to over-consume defense spending are attenuated. And of course the free rider problem would be likewise lessened relative to an anarchist society. The probable result of such a policy is a more rational level of defense spending than either the current extreme or the anarchist extreme would produce.

For example, since the central government cannot issue its own debt, but must ask for borrowing through the states, the tactic of taxing someone else to pay for defense spending would be much harder. And this debt would not be in funny money that governments can produce at will, but real money. State governments are going to be very reluctant to issue more debt for federal officials to spend- especially since in localism political parties which run candidates for Federal Office cannot run candidates for state or local offices and vice-versa. State and federal officials will no longer be part of the same club.

It is also so that in a localist nation there are no federal ground forces. They are all borrowed from the states. Politicians from one state will find it much harder to vote to tax all of the others to fund a weapons system that is built in their state. Instead, the payer and the beneficiary will be the same. Thus resources will be allocated rationally.

This section, while placed under arguments against anarchist's ideas, applies equally to central state spending. Much like each view is an opposite extreme based on an imbalanced view of private threats vs. public threats to individual liberty, these philosophies also produce opposite extremes and erroneous outcomes on the amount of money spent on the classic public use goods. The anarchist society will grossly under-consume such goods, resulting in an inability to preserve their society (which might explain why no such societies exist as sovereigns in the modern world).

Conversely, if the ruling elites of a central state don't siphon off the wealth of the populace via some other means, the central state will grossly *over-consume* such spending, until the debt and misallocation of resources also threatens the prosperity and freedom of such a society.

Anarchist Societies and Fiat Currency

Anyone who has read and understood *Localism, A Philosophy of Government* is aware of the grave threat that fiat currency poses to a free society. No people can remain free so long as an oligarchy controls the issue of their currency. Fiat currency is the means by which the elites have expropriated our wealth and government- leveraging the future earnings of our own children to capitalize the insidious devices by which our serfdom is forged. Localism not only recognizes this threat, but makes deliberate provision against it.

In contrast, anarchist societies have no defense against fiat currency. As far as I can tell, this weakness has not been explored in anarchist literature and thought. On the problems of defense spending and police protection they have at least produced answers, unsatisfactory and impractical though they might be. When it comes to the threat to free societies posed by fiat currencies however, anarchists don't even show any awareness of the problem, much less present viable solutions.

Perhaps there is a reason for this. They may not see the threat because their own society would have no government to impose a fiat currency on them. It takes a government to establish a fiat currency, or at the least, a government to force the acceptance of one. But as will be shown here, it also takes a government to protect a society from the risk of infection by the fiat currency of *other* nations. This is a threat for which anarchist theorems posit no solution. Even if they can somehow manage to protect themselves from the foreign sword, against the foreign printing press they find themselves defenseless.

What gives the Dollar, the Euro, or the Yuan value? The root of their value is in force. So long as the governments of those nations have legal tender laws, those bits of fiat paper can be used to purchase anything those huge and talented populations make. So thanks to force, those bits of paper do have value. Not intrinsic value perhaps, but imputed value due to the force behind their mandated acceptance. This may not be just, it may violate the Non-Aggression Principle, but fiat money has value so long as the government enforces legal tender laws.

Cotton picked by slaves still has value. If you get robbed at gunpoint the stolen items still have value. And items bought with fiat money from a population required by law to accept it also have value. So even if the citizens of an anarchist society have no fiat currency of their own imposed on them personally, they still have an incentive through self-interest to accept the fiat currency of other nations as payment.

It is true that the citizens of an anarcho-capitalist society will not be *forced* to accept fiat currency. They won't have to be forced though, they will accept it willingly. Once one hundred million productive people are forced to take a fiat currency, the rest of the world doesn't have to be forced. They willingly take it because they know those people will be forced to take it. It has value imputed to it by government force.

Nor will it matter if some or even most members of the anarcho-capitalist paradise refuse to take the fiat. The issuers of the fiat will simply trade with those who will accept it until the rest throw in the towel, or are bought out with trade items bought with fiat.

Some might reply that one response would be to boycott people and businesses which accept fiat currency. The threat of organizing a boycott against those who accept Euros is an empty one when the other side starts with 360 million people (in the case of the Euro) plus whatever proportion of your population who will take the Euro right away. In fact, the head start is much larger because the other nations who have their own fiat will accept them as well.

The rational choice, based on self-interest, for any business and certainly any individual is to say "yes" to the fiat world in preference to the sliver of the national population who would seriously stick with a boycott. They will be worn down in time anyway.

It is always state intervention which eventually acts to reduce transactions of this nature, be it ending slavery or enforcing laws against "theft by receiving" stolen property. Individuals may benefit from getting stolen goods at a discount, or goods produced under slave conditions at a discount. It is to their personal advantage, just like accepting fiat is.

Notice I did not say that accepting fiat was the rational choice for the long-term health of your society as a whole. I think quite the opposite. These are examples of where what is good for the individual is bad for society as a whole. The long term consequence of fiat currency is the corruption and destruction of whatever real economy you had as wealth becomes increasingly concentrated into the hands of those closest to the printing presses.

That dear readers, is why we must have the state. We must have the state to protect ourselves from others who have states. Not just for military reasons, but to protect ourselves from the more insidious and even harder to resist means of conquest to be found in the scourge of fiat money.

Once all the real wealth around you has been bought up with paper by those few who control the presses, you can't stay free in any meaningful sense of the word. You can't remain stateless in any meaningful sense of the word, because whatever private security firm they run will become effectively the new state security force. They will have the resources to either buy-out or rub out their potential competitors.

The evidence for this outcome abounds. Just look at what has happened to America in a single lifetime. When I was born, our currency was not fiat. America's paper money could be exchanged for gold by foreigners (at $35 per ounce), and for silver coin by citizens. By the time I was ten years old, that had changed. Now the gold is gone from our money and the silver is gone from our money. It has been replaced by debt, which the financial class says that we owe to them.

History shows us that governments invariably try to escape any obligations attached to the currency which they issue. When government issues its own money, it will eventually try to reduce, and if it can escape altogether, the obligation to back that money with something of value. In my childhood, history repeated itself. By 1972, the government of the United States escaped all its obligations to back its currency with monetary metal and the dollar became a fiat currency.

Now, in my fifties, I see the middle class is a shell of its former self. Whereas when I was a child one spouse working could provide a decent living for most families, now we see households are struggling to stay in the middle class with both spouses working (when they can find work) and piles of debt. We have gone from the largest creditor nation in the world, with everyone owing us money, to the largest debtor nation in history, with us owing others staggering sums which we have no means to ever repay. All of this in the lifetime of one man.

The wealth of America has not vanished, it has simply moved from the hands of the general citizenry into the hands of those closest to the pressmasters. In its place we are left with the debt they used to create the currency. The wealth of this nation has been removed from the many and concentrated in the hands of the special few. These gained it not by merit, or by talent, or by service, as honest wealth is gained, but rather through the fraud of fiat money. And this result is being repeated in other nations, confirming the truth of the matter.

We may all see how governments reduce economic injustice by prosecuting people for receiving stolen property. The reason we can't see this same positive effect in their currency interventions is that they are presently using their power not to eliminate injustice, but to eliminate the competition in an injustice which the ruling class is perpetrating on its citizens.

That is, when a government with fiat currency insists on an exchange rate at the border and limits the amount of foreign currency one can bring into or out of the country, it is not doing so to eliminate scams, but rather to eliminate all *other* such scams, in favor of the scam that *they* are running. They want to increase demand for their kind of paper by restricting the use of the other gang's type of paper. The domestic market is where they can get away with using the most muscle to keep the other gang's paper out. And of course if they keep enough of it out, then fewer people bother to accept it, reducing its market value even further relative to their own paper.

Because of this the efforts of governments to control the flow of various currencies (currency controls) are usually a bad thing, a criminal scheme to force more undeserved value into the brand of paper they are pushing. But if a government cannot issue its own currency, nor pick and choose among any private currencies which are backed by monetary metals, then any power to control what fiat currencies are allowed cannot be used to advance its own interests over those of its citizens. It has no dog in the steal-via-fiat race.

If a government cannot loot its citizens in this manner, its next most self-interested position is to protect its citizens from such looting by other governments. It is only within these very limited circumstances that currency controls can be a good thing.

I am under no illusions about the intrinsic virtue of government or those who staff it. Governments are institutions and when institutions are large enough, they take on a life of their own. Those who run them have interests and goals apart from those that the institution was originally created to serve. Regardless of whatever motivation a large institution was established to serve, the first cause and calling of any successful bureaucracy is its own well-being. The structure of government originally built to protect people's rights and property can eventually become the biggest threat to them, and through a multitude of devices fleece them of their wealth.

First among the ways governments fleece wealth from people is through the use of fake money. The first and last impulse of every government will be to use its power to create its own currency so that the process of subtly looting the population through currency debasement can begin anew. It is a choice which must be firmly denied to them.

It should be made crystal clear to government that their first choice about money, create their own currency to initiate the process of looting the populace through eventual debasement, is out of their reach. If the self-interested state apparatus understands that it cannot play such a game, it will default to its second self-interested preference. This will be to prevent any other governments from playing such a game on their turf.

If government is running its own stereo-fencing operation, then its efforts to keep other such groups out does not really help protect the citizens from stereo theft. In such a case the government is just trying to maximize its gains from theft, not protect the citizens from theft. It is only when government is not in the stereo-fencing business that its efforts to stop such activities actually represent an attempt to benefit the public, rather than whoever runs their own such operation.

In the same way, a government with no power to make currency can't pursue its first interest so it defaults to its second- which is to defend the population from attempts by others to do what it would do had it the power. Notice we are not counting on government being pure in this matter. Rather we are limiting its options so that the interests of the government and the general good of the population are the same. Banned from looting us themselves in this manner, their next best way to preserve their power lies in keeping the nation free from the fiat schemes of others and saying "If we can't loot them, then nobody can."

To become and remain a free and just society, we have to get government out of the money-creating business. On that Anarcho-capitalists and Localists can agree. Where we differ is on how our society can protect itself from the fiat currency of other nations. Because it is to the advantage of the individual to take such currency even when it is to the disadvantage of the whole of society, the government must act to restrict fiat currency "invasions" in order to preserve freedom.

There is a commonality here with "public use" goods (goods which have benefits that individuals cannot be excluded from) like defense spending. That is, it is to the advantage of each individual to donate less to defense spending than they might really know to be their fair share because they benefit from defense whether they pay their full share or not. They cannot be excluded from the benefits even if they don't pay the full costs. In a similar manner, the gain to the individual for accepting fiat currency is immediate and theirs alone, while the costs of such a decision are put off and spread amongst the whole society.

Anarcho-capitalists don't have a means to protect any society they might build from the corrosive effects of force-backed fiat money. The only counter that will work long-term is a force-backed *ban* of such money. One might say that the free market should decide what money might be used, but there is no freedom in how government fiat money gains its value. It is gained by compulsion. There is no free market in how the value was gained, only in how it is traded once gained, much like the stolen stereo.

Where water is not available, fire must be fought with fire. Sadly, in order to preserve as free a society as possible, the contagion of force-backed fiat currency must be kept out by force – the force of government. If someone initiates force, and uses it in a way that is harmful to you, using force in return is recognized as a legitimate response, even by anarchists.

When the press masters of a fiat currency buy up the wealth of your nation with force-backed money, they are using that force against you. Not directly perhaps, but indirectly by turning the force they used against their own populations into a means to economically dominate your society. In a society without government economic dominance is societal dominance.

The Limits of Private Currencies

"*Money is gold, nothing else!*" – J.P. Morgan testifying before Congress in 1912.

There is one more thing which ought to be mentioned here. *Localism, A Philosophy of Government* was penned before private fiat currencies like Bitcoin gained traction. Localism does permit governments to tax or ban fiat currencies whether public or private. The only sort of money which is protected from government intervention are forms of money which have the economic properties of natural money.

That is, it should be portable, durable, divisible, valuable (in itself, even if it were not being used as money), hard to counterfeit, and yet easy to store. It should be able to price goods in terms of a single number, such as "1 troy ounce of pure silver". Another way of saying this is that its units should be uniform in value. One unit of a given size should be of equal value as all other units of that size. It should be a store of value and a medium of exchange.

Essentially, many metals fit this full list and not much else does. Metals are naturals for the role of money. Most other items don't fit the full list for one reason or another. Diamonds for example, fit almost everything on the list, but they fail to meet the uniform value test- two diamonds of the same size can have greatly different values. They are also hard to divide. There is really not much else besides metals which can fit the whole list.

Almost anything however, can be securitized. One can have a piece of paper representing a ton of pork bellies, or West Texas Intermediate Crude, or, in the case of Bitcoin, nothing physical at all. And if two people wish to barter and exchange such items then of course they should be allowed to do so. Localism's provision allowing government to tax or ban inferior currencies (those lacking the qualities of natural money listed above and found in many economics text-books) is not a prohibition on barter between individuals.

Barter is a direct exchange of goods without the use of a medium (a currency). Localism maintains that legitimate mediums for exchange are those which would have value even were they not used as a currency. Where Localism makes allowances for state intervention is in the case of fiat- a currency unit which has little or no value in itself, only value because some agree that it is to be used as money. This illusion opens the door to fraud, even if the fraud is backed by human greed and gullibility rather than force in the case of government-backed fiat.

But what public interest is served when the state has the power to tax or ban a Bitcoin? Why must government retain the potential to restrict money to its natural form (goods that would have value even if they were not being used as money), rather than let anything whose value is not imputed by force serve as money?

The short answer is that it is a matter of national and economic security. It is a necessary measure to protect the freedom of a nation and the freedom of those within it from threats similar to those posed by force-backed fiat currency.

As of this writing, Bitcoin is still highly successful, but cracks are beginning to show. Perhaps by the time you read this Bitcoin will have already been sent to the dust-bin of history, but something like it is sure to rise in its place. The allure of money from nothing, of value plucked from the ether without effort, and the magic of electronic alchemy will insure its rebirth no matter how hard the lessons of history have been on our forebears.

In honest money value must be put into the money first. Efforts to ascribe value to something as money where no real value is present is fraud. Fraud which many willingly believe due to human frailty and greed, but fraud none the less. Fiat money is but a Ponzi scheme where the users are also the used and everyone thinks they are in on the scam until the end. That rascal Voltaire noted long ago that "paper money eventually returns to its intrinsic value- zero." Private paper (or electronic) money is no exception to this rule. Indeed without the backing of government force this process will only be accelerated.

But I do wonder if the users of Bitcoin have noticed that even though present governments have the power to tax or ban its use, they have not done so. One wonders if the selling points of anonymity and security are only temporary illusions. That is, governments know how to trace these transactions, and know how to raid accounts. Shutting Bitcoin down would be like shutting down a gangster's nightclub that was thoroughly bugged. They could do it, but they would lose a lot of valuable information that way.

Bitcoin seems desirable now because the alternative is government-backed fiat. Localists want a society where private money reigns supreme, with the government only allowed to intervene to stop the use of money backed by force or fraud. Fiat currency from other governments is backed by force, and private fiat is backed by fraud. The fraud is that the money is represented as having value when no real value is present. As an aside, I reject the argument that intrinsic value is an illusion, at least on a practical basis. Any theory which would ascribe equal intrinsic value to Michelangelo's *David* and a lump of granite is missing something.

One may say that the purchasers of Bitcoin know that it holds no intrinsic value, that it relies on the confidence and trust of the system to impute value. Exactly- the value is not there. It is an agreed-on illusion, one that history shows will burst, harming not only those who bought in, but if the collapse is big enough, our whole economy. In one's head one can know that a private fiat holds no real value, but the allure of a marketing campaign and the promise that you won't be the one holding the bag when reality asserts itself simply draws victims in via greed, the normal tool of the con-man.

It is easy to imagine a scenario where the Goldman-Sachs and J.P. Morgans of the world start their own version of bitcoin. It would have the favor of every government that they already own. They could put a slick marketing campaign behind it to draw in wide acceptance and "confidence". And in time, the use of such a currency could overwhelm the real money in the economy as the vast majority of transactions come to be made with the private fiat of the same global banks which once controlled the nations with "public" fiat.

At that point, no matter who you elect, they would be at the mercy of the same people that run things now. They could crash your nation's economy at any time simply by pulling the rug out from under their private currency. Then, with your economy crashed, they simply buy things up at pennies on the dollar with real money, which they slowly acquired using the fiat currency whose value was an illusion.

The odds are that they would never have to execute this plan though. Simply the threat of executing this plan would be enough to wrench most governments into line. No politician wants to be on watch when the economy crashes. Merely the threat of the great banks doing so would induce political leaders to continue to alter the laws in their favor, regardless of any constitutional impediments to the change. Thus over time, one rule change at a time, they could affect a subtle take-over of the nation. This is what happens now with the government-backed private fiat currency called the dollar.

I understand that there will be many who do not want to be convinced by these arguments. It is very hard to convince someone with mere facts and logic to turn down what they think is access to easy money. It can also be disappointing to learn that not all principles of good government can be condensed down into a paragraph or two. I can only implore such readers to enthrone their rational principle, their logos, above any emotional desire to believe that all questions of the limits of a just government can be condensed into a few paragraphs.

I can only appeal to reason over greed when explaining the benefits of insisting that individuals in a society use just money rather than illusory money. We don't really create new wealth when we agree to impute value to fiat money, only the illusion of it, which is a form of fraud. The value must be put into the money up front. It must be contained in the money, not imputed to it by a mutual agreement that the Emperor's new clothes are very splendid indeed.

In micro-economic terms it may be no skin off your nose if someone down the block loses their savings when a fiat money scheme collapses. One may think "Let the buyer beware, they should not have been so foolish." But in macro-economic terms if the scheme was big enough it hurts everyone when it blows up, even those not fooled. Because of this, the temptation will be strong for those in charge to intervene and keep it from blowing up- via means similar to the criminal 2008 bank bail outs and Quantitative Easing. The current financial class knows all too well how to use "too big to fail" to their advantage.

With a JP Morgan behind it, a private fiat could go on for a generation, making anyone who does not jump in a fool. Once they pull the plug, it will be anyone who does not jump out that will be a fool. The insiders will know when that is, you will not. Such games are hard to play with real money.

This leaves only one question, and that concerns currency which is backed, not by metal, but by other things, such as crude oil or toilet paper, or any other real good. Such a currency would have some real value. Why should governments retain the power to ban or tax their use?

If there is a reasonable relationship to the value of the currency and the value of the product backing it, governments ought to leave it be. The true purpose of the prohibition was to prevent such currencies from using a nominal amount of real goods to pinch-hit for a fiat currency of much greater worth. For example, a currency redeemable for one gallon of crude oil set to a value such that it could purchase five gallons is not really a crude oil backed currency. It is just a fiat currency with a nominal amount of real goods as a cover.

Since crude oil does not meet all the true properties of natural money, people will tend not to redeem the currency for the good which backs it as readily as they would, for example, gold or silver backed currency. This makes it extremely easy for the issuers of such currency to not only leverage but overleverage. This amounts to yet another way false value can be created out of thin air.

If the issuers of a fiat currency maintain stocks of real goods in sufficient quantity to fully back their currency, and if the seniorage of such a currency is reasonable, then such a currency does not corrupt an economy and the government should allow it without penalty. Should either of these conditions fail, then in self-defense against the corrosive influence of fake money, the government retains the right to intervene with a tax or even a ban of such currency.

The Case Against Anarchism

Let me then sum up the case against Anarchism in only a few pages. The localist case against Anarchism begins with the philosophy. If the philosophy is flawed, it is highly unlikely that the prescriptions which flow from that philosophy will be right. Much space was spent demonstrating that the cornerstones of anarchist thought, Self-ownership, Symmetry, and Delegation, are not necessarily true.

A summation of our proofs would be thus: if a Creator God exists who has a higher moral order which applies to the state, then none of those ideas (Self-ownership, Symmetry, or Delegation) need be strictly true, and if no Creator God exists then all truth becomes meaningless or at least relative. The term "rights" in such a case has no objective meaning. In either case, it is demonstrated that there is no rational necessity to treat the premises supporting anarchy as true.

The next section of the defense against Anarchism pondered how much freedom the Creator wants humans to have, or put in non-theistic terms, "what is the ideal amount of freedom." Anarchists view the answer as a fixed and vast amount. As regards God's perfect will, as it applies to conditions in Heaven, I agree. On earth though, there appears to be a dynamic relationship between the virtue of a population and the amount of freedom which they can safely possess. This is a disturbing thought, but that does not make it untrue, nor am I the first to note it- many of the Founders believed themselves that our Constitution was made only for a moral and religious people.

The Bill of Rights might only be a starting point for the rights and freedoms a worthy population should be entitled to. For a debauched, violence-prone, and dishonest people even the Bill of Rights would be too much freedom for them to safely hold. See the population of any prison for an example. What might they do to one another, were not their freedoms extremely curtailed? A virtuous population is the best defense against big government.

The over-riding theme is that the anarchist philosophy does not work in a fallen world. It fails to protect people from lawless threats both within and exterior to any anarchist society. Police and in particular Military protection constitute "Public Use Goods" which will be grossly under-consumed when mandatory taxation is forbidden. Public Use Goods will be over-consumed in the central state, but two wrongs don't make a right. A prosperous and free anarchist society could not adequately defend itself against central states tempted to loot them.

Finally, I showed that an even greater threat than military conquest is economic corruption via force-backed fiat currency. Anarchism simply has no defense against this dire threat to freedom. What is in the self-interest of the free individual accrues to the ultimate demise of the free society. We must all agree to give up some economic freedom in order to preserve all the rest of economic freedom for us all.

The bumper-sticker anarchist response of "If man can't rule himself properly then how can a government of men rule others?" is wholly neutered by these evidences. Even if men are equal in the sense that they have the same rights, men are not equal in their ability to rule themselves, or in their ability to govern others. Some lack the virtue to properly rule even themselves. The prisons are full of men who could not successfully rule themselves, even were they under the truncated anarchist legal code. Indeed I was not so good at ruling myself at age twenty-one as I am now.

On the other hand, some men are so virtuous that not only might they govern themselves well, but for a time at least they might also govern at least some others well. Every successful parent is an example of this type.

This is not to say that there is a ruling class whose superiority somehow entitles them to unchecked power. All government power should have multiple checks on it. We are all fallen humans who at some point need restraint both by that which governs us and in that which we govern. The better humans we are, the less of that we will need, until one day we might hope that the need for the state fades like a bad dream. Until that day comes, Localism presents our best hope in finding the maximum amount of freedom possible in a fallen world without setting in motion forces which result in the eventual loss of even more freedom.

Section Two: Localism against the Central State

Overview Against the Extremism of the Central State

"When plunder becomes a way of life for a group of men living together in society, they create for themselves in the course of time a legal system that authorizes it and a moral code that justifies it." - Frederic Bastiat

Let's now turn our attention to the opposite extreme which opposes the centrist and moderate view of localism. Whereas Anarchism is the extreme which puts too much faith in the individual man, belief in the Central State is the other extreme. It is an extreme which puts too much faith in that institution called the state. Or rather, in most cases the faith of those who believe in the central state is placed in some sort of elite which they suppose is made of finer clay than the rest of mankind. An elite to which many advocates for the central state most naturally assume that they belong.

To loosely paraphrase Bastiat, when men desire great power over other men badly enough, they typically devise a moral code which justifies these actions and desires. Because of this, almost all elites are on some level ideological elites. Most believe they are better than the rest of mankind, that they have a right or duty to rule over mankind. In modern times this is often based on ideology. That is, they subscribe to some philosophy which is so superior and will bring such benefits that it justifies their imposing it on everyone with or without their consent.

There are of course exceptions in the length of history. Royalty and nobles who held to "the Divine Right of Kings" as a philosophy likely began with the belief that it was something in their person, not their ideas, which gave them the right to rule. The philosophy came later, in recognition of that prior belief. In more modern times, the Nazis combined a belief that they had a right or duty to rule in their persons, because they were of the Master Race, with a belief that they had a right to rule within this Master Race because of their superior ideology. The Germans would rule the world, and the Nazi Party would rule the Germans.

My observation is that this sense of hubris and entitlement is very common in the upper echelons of any centralized system, be it militant Islam, Christian Dominionists, Communists, or whatever the label may be. At the bottom, such movements tend to be dominated by the insecure, unthoughtful, and unaccomplished. These are persons who crave a sense of certainty even if based on illusion, and live vicariously through allegiance to their cause.

Most humans have an innate desire to be a part of something larger than themselves. There is, so to speak, a "God shaped hole" built into the human soul which is filled when that soul is connected to a higher cause. When used positively, this feature of the human psyche has led many people to seek a life of peace, holiness, and continual self-improvement in the course of service to others. While this innate human need was perhaps intended to facilitate connection to our Maker, men are prone to fill it with other things.

Fallen as we are, we take this innate desire to be a part of something larger than ourselves, meant to be a good thing, and fill it with something else which may or may not be good. I am a fan of higher causes myself, but only with the understanding that they are shadows of the type- the highest higher cause to which other noble causes must take second place.

Every caring person has their causes, but what are the characteristics of their first cause? Is it to become better themselves or is it to make some individual(s) in their life better off? Or is it to make "the world" or some other such collective better? Not all causes are equal in their ability to do good, or to do harm.

There are those who seek to glorify the state, or a political party, or some other such cause, and abuse this feature of humanity in order to do so. This is done by offering the state, or the party, or whatever cause they champion as the entity which ought to fill this hole in man's soul. They offer some Collective as the First Cause for which the individual should give themselves up. That is, they attempt to substitute their cause, in the case of Statists then the state, for that which was meant to be there.

In the long run of course, the innate need will not be fulfilled by substitutes. The individual will be let down, because giving one's self for the state or the party or what have you cannot forever fill a hole meant to be filled by intimacy with one's Maker. Of course we humans don't live in the long run, we live in the "now."

What might induce someone to accept the weak substitute of a state or a party as one's higher cause? A common reason is that the substitute permits one to hang onto, or even celebrate, certain moral failings, whereas the genuine calling would eventually force one to abandon them. For example, if a German in the 1930s did not care for Jews or Slavs, nor for pious living, he might have to repent of these dispositions to fill his God-shaped hole with God. Should the same man seek to fill this void with fascism and the Nazi party, these same dispositions would be celebrated.

The temptation for every person is to seek out a false "higher calling"- one which allows them to indulge whatever vices or moral failings which they might already have. They need not change hating who they hate, or loving what they love. A common characteristic of a dangerous higher calling is that the world must change, but not them! False calls accommodate what is false in the man answering the call, while a true call prompts men to reject that which is false in themselves.

Demanding that one's enemies yield, or change, or be defeated is an easier higher calling than one which would instead guide us unto a course of continual self-assessment and moral improvement. By this game man plays with himself, the need to lose one's self in a higher cause is fulfilled while man deftly avoids what the sages tell us is the true purpose for which the need was placed in the human heart to begin with.

Those who would offer the State as a substitute higher calling are well aware of this weakness in human character. They will take what is meant to be a good thing for the individual, this inclination we have by Divine order to want to belong to a greater purpose than ourselves, and pervert it to unjust ends.

Only in a few cases, such as communism, does the state reject the concept of God outright. The more common approach is to claim the name and the authority of the gods for themselves. Tyrants have since the rise of the central state itself tried to either make gods of their leaders, or co-opt the name of God on behalf of the state. All the better to get a closer counterfeit to the God-shaped hole in the human heart. In such a case, the gods become mere mascots for the state.

The default setting for the Christian Church over the last thousand years of western civilization is to urge citizens to obey the secular laws. That is the default setting, but the default setting is not the only setting. Even in the Book of Acts, in the first days of the Christian Church, we see that when secular leaders go too far the apostles tell them "we must obey God rather than men."

It is no accident of history that the nations which most advanced human liberty were those which embraced Christianity. It is a paradox that a religion whose scriptures teach cooperation and submission to government authorities is also that religion which has most been associated with the advancement of human liberty and the rejection of tyrannical government.

There is something about a focus on improving the individual first which makes people self-governing to a degree that it makes tyranny untenable. Tyranny is overcome best by first renewing the mind of the citizens so that they have no need of tyrants to compel them to cooperate with their neighbors for good. Not even mighty Rome was able to overcome this peaceful revolution, though they had quenched countless uprisings before.

The default setting under this view of God and man is cooperation with the state. However the default setting is not the only setting, and an increasingly good population puts continuous pressure on a government less virtuous than itself.

When a religion has no setting other than the default setting of obedience to the state; when obedience to the gods and obedience to the state becomes one and the same; then you may know that both church and state have become corrupted with the ultimate corruption- the desire to set up the political machinery of man as a false god.

This describes the mind-set of many of those who worship at the altar of the central state. As an aside, because it is a mind-set prone to moral imbalance- i.e. extremism, it can also describe the mind of some anarchists, whose nominal cause is "liberty." "Liberty" can become the cover for demands that one's moral failings be accommodated. In my view many moral failings should be accommodated by the government for the sake of liberty, but those who obsess on using liberty for ignoble purpose will not long retain it, whatever their demands.

Still, we have spent a great deal of time focusing on the shortcomings of anarchism in the previous section. This section is meant to discuss the short-comings of those who believe in the central state. Let us continue on that subject.

The General Categories of Advocates for the Central State

"Virtually no idea is too ridiculous to be accepted, even by very intelligent and highly educated people, if it provides a way for them to feel special and important. Some confuse that feeling with idealism." - Thomas Sowell

Central state adherents generally fall into three categories. One of these categories is the elites. These are those who believe they are part of a special and exalted subset of humanity, and because they are they are justified in gathering up all power into their own hands. Because they were much-discussed in the previous chapter, they need not be addressed in detail here.

A second group is the unthoughtful. These are those who gladly out-source their individual conscience and decision-making to the collective run by those elites. George Bernard Shaw once noted that "Liberty means responsibility. That is why most men dread it." Choosing a party, or a country, or whatever other collective one might belong to, and uncritically accepting whatever the leaders of this collective say is a means of evading the dreadful part of liberty. It is a lazy way of pretending to preserve one's freedom without having to fulfill the dreaded "responsibility" part which Mr. Shaw mentioned.

It doesn't work if the goal is really protecting freedom, but it manages a facade of doing so. If one knows that one has civic duties, then one can pretend they are fulfilled by performing this ritual. It's a sort of fig-leaf for the conscience. It also provides the unthoughtful with a team to cheer for in an elaborate parody of self-government.

Thinking is hard work, and acting on those thoughts can be harder. Especially when a matter does not seem to be of immediate concern. The central state offers a solution for all those who fear the responsibilities which accompany liberty. It offers a solution for those who are whipped into a frenzy of fear over some foreign bogeyman. It offers a solution for those who like most of us simply want to be a little lazy. Central experts at the capitol or party head-quarters will take care of all of those things for us, we need only give uncritical assent to their Master Plans.

People in a society who wish to be unthoughtful will find that there are those who will volunteer to do their thinking for them. Humans can be induced to succumb to this temptation through laziness, through fear, or lack of confidence, or a preference for a moral system offered by some elite over that of their own conscience. In most of the present world, inertia also factors into the equation. Because the extremism of the central state is what we currently have, a slice of this group will not be fans if the central state *per se*, put rather are simply uncomfortable with change. They want what is, because it is.

Besides the Elites and the Unthoughtful, there are those who support the central state solely out of self-interest. They support the system regardless of its abuses because they believe the get more out of it than they put into it. Whatever sense of guilt they might have regarding the system's looting of innocent persons is over-ridden by the knowledge that they are in on the looting.

This group supports centralized government power because they fear that if it were otherwise their slaves may too easily get away! A localist prefers government power as decentralized as is practicable precisely so that those dissatisfied with their government might be able to escape its authority as easily and cheaply as possible.

I refer to those who support centralized government power primarily because they think they can loot more than they get looted as “those whose god is their own belly”, or GITOBs. The morality of the government's actions is less relevant to them than their own interests and appetites.

There is overlap in motivations among these three categories. Elitists can also be GITOBs. Often they are doing well by doing “good” in government “service”. The Unthoughtful might also be GITOBs because they don't want to think about the fact that their income is derived in part from laying more debt on unborn children, who have no vote with which to defend themselves from what I call “Generational Looting”.

It therefore comes to be that we have a citizenry who identify themselves with their state to an unhealthy degree. The first group (the elites) might lead the nation into one unnecessary conflict after another, such as an effort to impose our values and systems on foreign cultures at gunpoint. The second group (the unthoughtful) might cheer on their military like a fan cheers on their favorite sports team- disassociated from an honest appraisal of the morality or immorality of any given military action. And members of the third group (GITOBS) just want the government spending to continue, because they get a piece of it.

A Different Sort of Approach

"It is difficult to get a man to understand something when his salary depends on his not understanding it." - Upton Sinclair

The central state is a giant racket where those close to the beast can strip wealth from those less connected to it with a minimum of effort. I could write five hundred pages of well-documented evidence from history to show how bad, and how dangerous, states with large central governments can be and have been. I could do that, and such books have been written. I won't bother trying to write another because those who favor the central state do so for very different reasons than many of those who favor anarchy.

In the latter case, there exists at least the pretense of reason. There is a consistent philosophy behind anarchist ideas and thus one is able to answer with philosophical arguments of one's own. Many adherents of the central state have a vested interest in not understanding arguments against the central state. It is not a problem of the intellect, but a problem of the will.

When this is the problem, questioning one's philosophy will simply lead you on a frustrating journey with no destination.

They will throw up flimsy ideas which could not withstand the least scrutiny and then aggressively resist their being scrutinized. When the real problem is will, one must call people on their intentions, not their arguments.

Will those who want a central state because they see themselves as part of an elite with a master plan for the rest of humanity be keen to understand why they should endorse Localism? That is, embrace a framework for government which is designed to stop people exactly like them? They won't reject it because it's a bad idea, they will reject it because it conflicts with their ambitions. Again, the real issue is the will, not the intellect.

And what of those who literally depend on the government for their salary, or welfare check, or however their loot is labeled? Are they really interested in which philosophy of government brings the most liberty to mankind? Most will be primarily interested in a philosophy which keeps the loot coming, be it in the form of welfare checks or government contracts. Whatever fig-leafs they may advance to justify making their neighbors into virtual debt-slaves for their own benefit are not the real issue.

In such cases, resolving what is the real issue is will not be a question of education. It is not a question of presenting the arguments in a form that they might be better understood. Lack of understanding is not the real issue. Their will is the issue. When will is the issue, there is no persuading.

A second important reason why I need not delve into the level of detail I did with anarchy with regards to arguments against the central state is that we live in an age of large central states. Thoughtful and observant people are already aware of the flaws and problems with the central state. It is very likely that part of the reason you selected this book is because you already sense the current arrangement of things is deeply flawed.

Bearing in mind all of the above, in the following pages I will present a few of the best philosophical and logical arguments against the central state. There are plenty of other approaches, such as expounding on the particular failures of central planning and big government which we can find daily. What I want to focus on is not some particular instance of state failure, but why, if the goal is human freedom, the central state must *always* fail.

Rational Ignorance and Irrational Education in the Central State

It has been pointed out by many commentators that if you view the political choices of a typical citizen from a cost-benefit analysis then it becomes apparent that it is not really worth an individual's time to make an informed choice for President, or any other large office. A single voter will simply have too little say in the outcome to make the time and effort required for a proper choice worth the trouble. The rational person in this case would not find it worth their while to vote. This is especially true when both of the two “choices” agree on many key policies.

This argument has been used by anarchists as a point against all republican or democratic forms of government. They reason that since it is not worth an individual person's time to choose, why give voting for one's rulers any credibility? According to this line of thinking, the election system is a sham designed to give people the appearance or feeling that they have a say in things while in reality their wishes are subsumed by the collective.

The prime example of this theory is the presidency. Many if not most voters, driven by around-the-clock media coverage, spend most of their political energy in the race for President of the United States. That is the least rational place to expend one's political efforts, since the influence any one of us would have in that race is weak. Meanwhile many of those same voters are not even aware of who the candidates are for their state or county legislative seats.

The "rational ignorance" theory suggests that people pay much more attention to who their insurance company is than who ought to be on their city council. The "rational ignorance" concept is thus used by anarchists as an argument for replacing all government with private security firms, which would operate somewhat like private insurance firms.

While some evidence supports this line of reasoning, it is not an argument against all elective government. Rather, it is an argument against large and centralized direct elective government. It is an argument against stacking all the power in one national office in a distant city. It is a decent argument, even if it neglects the truth that people do not always make rational allocations of their time and efforts.

The political system has attempted to short-circuit this quandary by taking effort out of the equation for most voters. That is, they set up two choices representing two known brands, and have citizens pick between those two. The problem of "rational ignorance" is evaded by limiting the choice so much that little thought is required to distinguish which one any particular voter might prefer. One could be cheerfully ignorant, rationally ignorant, and still cast one's vote because the choice was made so limited and easy that little self-education was required.

For many decades, this scheme has worked. Voters went with the label they liked and little thought or effort was required on their part in selecting which of the two choices they would vote for. They convinced themselves that as long as they participated in this ritual, they were fulfilling their obligations as a good citizen.

Expect some persons to resent being presented with other options. There are people who want to cling to the illusion that their bi-annual ceremony at the ballot box is enough. What they want to believe is that their duty ends there, and by so doing they are still free and leaving a self-governing society to their children. For them "rational ignorance" is their preferred condition. It permits them the illusion that all they need do is continue their red-team or blue-team cheerleading. That is the other face of the "rationally ignorant".

When things seemed to be going well for the nation, this farce played out beautifully. Dissatisfaction with the scheme is growing as it becomes more apparent that those who are close to the top of the two large private political clubs which control ballot access are using it to loot the country for themselves and the interests which fund them.

It is now apparent that the idea of outsourcing our ballot access mechanism to a party label managed in a distant city and funded by global corporations is a failed model. The evidence for this is overwhelming and conclusive. We need to revert to self-government. The path to do so is suggested in the "Third Pillar" of the book *Localism, a philosophy of government.*

While "rational ignorance" is a decent argument against the Central State, it does not apply to Localism. If one constructs the state as suggested in the pages of *Localism, a philosophy of government*, with the most power in local offices, then the cost-benefit analysis changes dramatically.

For local offices, the views of every citizen counts. Their opinion matters. Their vote matters. Their involvement in an election campaign matters. A single motivated citizen can do a lot to help a local candidate win, or lose, an election. For such a situation it makes sense to expend the effort necessary for an informed choice. It becomes very reasonable and worthwhile to vote and engage in self-rule when the local offices are the most important ones. Especially when government is stepping on your toes.

One might counter that the “rational ignorance” principle would still apply to whatever large offices were left in a localist nation. Indeed the accounting would favor ignorance even more since those offices would wield far less power than under a central state. To some extent this is true, but the Founders in America have already answered that one. Originally neither the federal Senate nor the Presidency were voted on directly. Rather, people voted for either state legislators or electors to do the research for them and make informed choices in their behalf. Self-government is thus preserved as a rational cost-benefit proposition.

Remember also that in Localism relations between governments are voluntary. States can leave nations, counties can leave states. Even if people don't spend a lot of time thinking about who is running national government, national government must still be responsive to the needs of states and local governments. In a localist nation these smaller governmental units are almost like “customers'” of the larger governments. Those “customers” will make sure the more central government is kept in line, and individual citizens will serve as “customers” for the local governments.

The rational ignorance argument may still stand against the central state. But it could only be a viable argument for anarchy if anarchy were a workable option for preserving rights in all other aspects. Sadly, it is not. Nation-states do provide some protections for their citizens which, despite idealized rationalizations, are not available by strictly private means.

Still, one of the arguments against the central state is that it is irrational for the average voter to care about informing themselves enough to make good choices. This is so, though the truth of it has been concealed by the modern central state via the construction of elaborate parodies of self-government where little citizen thought is required.

The Centralization of Government Power makes Collectivism Inevitable

In the end, the battle for what kind of government we want to have will come down to two basic positions. One side will be collectivist, and the other individualist. People who align with either of those two positions may wear various labels, but once you cut through the window dressing people either believe that most people should be free to run their own lives as they see fit, or that the common people will need direction from those "above" them. Either the default setting should favor the individual citizen, or it should favor the collective – guided of course by some elite group.

The honest labels of those who favor the collective are "leftist", "socialist", "liberal", "communitarian", and "fascist." The dishonest labels of those who favor the collective are "neo-conservative", and sometimes, "moderate." On the other side, those whose default setting is in favor of the individual, labels include some of the various anarchists, minarchist libertarians, classical liberals, constitutionalists, limited-government conservatives, and of course, localists. There is much philosophical overlap among these labels, but at the root of it all is this question of collectivism or the individual.

Excepting Anarchism which eschews government in *toto*, all of the other labels on the side of the individual are attempts to have the least amount of government possible while maintaining the order needed to preserve individual rights from Private Threats. Localism allows for each of those other answers (except anarchy) in various locales. Its main difference from the others is the degree of diligence allocated to the emplacement of barriers to the centralization of government power. These barriers are placed so that what starts as limited government may remain so. Just how limited it will be depends on the people of each locality.

Those of us who oppose collectivist answers must also oppose answers which centralize political and government power. The centralization of government power not only inevitably leads to the expansion of such powers, it also leads to collectivism. That centralizing government power leads to the expansion of such power is self-evident to even the casual student of history. I need not dwell on it here. Rather, I would like to elaborate on the other outcome of centralization- the transformation of the citizenry from individualists to collectivists.

When decisions are made locally, basically everybody is somebody. A citizen can stand before their city council, or county courts, and make his or her case as an individual and be heard on that basis. When power is centralized, the individual matters less. Their opinion does not count for much in consideration of which way the great wheels of state might turn.

Their best hope in such circumstances is to join with some group whose views mostly, but perhaps not completely, align with their own. By joining with the group, their voice will not be heard, but their voice will become a tiny part of a loud new voice which might be heard- that of a collective.

Once these collectives start forming up, it becomes even harder for an individual person to make their voice heard by the central state. The roar of the various collectives drown out the individual. And so it is that to have any part of their views heard at all, the citizen must cede the job of speaking to their government to these groups whose views are somewhat like their own, but yet not their own. The voice of the individual person is lost. Whatever nuance they might desire in some public policy will never get a hearing, even where that person lives. Such is the travesty of the collective.

Add to it that once a collective is formed, the beast has its own interests, which may be separate and apart from the desires of the members which it claims to represent. Does the National Right to Life for example, really want abortion to end in this nation? Maybe the organization has more to gain by keeping the controversy going than by attaining victory and shutting down. What about the NAACP? When every just grievance has been satisfied, how shall they justify their salaries? Once the collective gets a life of its own, it has its own interests, apart and separate from the interests of the individual persons who might join it or even the cause for which it was originally created to serve.

These special interest collectives often get "captured" by a larger collective, and thus their unique voice is lost just as that of their individual members was lost before them. An example of smaller collectives being caught up in a larger collective can be found in the numerous interest groups which get attached to one or the other national political parties. A national political party is in the large view simply another collective. They can and will co-opt as many of these groups as they can so that the real purpose of the group is subverted. Instead of holding the party accountable, they become mere excuse-makers for the party. That is one of the troubles with hierarchies.

And what do you suppose the effect of political "activism" of this sort has on the psyche of the citizens over time? They learn to think like members of a collective. They can easily forget to individually examine issues and instead take their cues from whatever large groups they have chosen to identify with. If the only real access to the system is through a collective, then individuals join collectives. They operate collectively, and in time whether they desire it or not, and whether they are even aware of it or not, they become *operational* collectivists.

How can this insidious process be circumvented? Localism provides the best answer. By confronting the key issue of centralization we confront the issue of collectivism. With the limitations on political parties that the theory advocates, the continual push towards collectivism is countered. Almost all decisions will be local ones, to be decided by the views of individual persons. And when individual rights are violated, the wronged person can look the decision-maker right in the eye and call them on it.

The only alternative to localism is centralization, which will result in all decisions being made by coalitions of collectives. In such a system individuals without the protection of a collective will be steam-rolled by massive bureaucracies in which no one person can even be shown to have responsibility for an offense. Therefore the battle against collectivism is a battle against centralization. To oppose collectivism is to support localism. Conversely, those in favor of the strong central state support collectivism whether they intend to or not.

Can Local Governments Do More Evil in Localism?

One of the very few pseudo-intellectual arguments which advocates for a central state have made against localism can be found in the charge that under it local governments will have more power to do what they consider "evil" than they imagine a centrally controlled state would do. The complaint is that without a strong central enforcement the aggrieved citizen will not be able to seek remedies for perceived injustices.

The answer of course is that they can obtain remedies. And not only that, their objections can actually be heard by the persons with the power to change the offending policy, since they are not hundreds of miles away and ringed by lobbyists (who most often are the ones who encouraged the politicians to enact the policy to which the citizen objects in the first place). When central governments "impose evil upon their society", it is both much harder to stop them and much harder to escape them.

Don't you see that the further removed the decision is from neighbors the easier it is to see them as faceless peasants? Your toes will be stepped on harder and more often if decisions are made centrally than if they are made locally. Not only will they be stepped on harder, and more often, and for less sensible purpose, but you will have less recourse if the decision to step on your toes is made centrally than if it is made locally.

Will that mean that more places will make decisions that you don't approve of? Maybe, but if one's philosophy is at all in accordance with moral reality there should also be more places that will make more decisions which one does approve of. Quite honestly it would not take much to improve on the current track record of government interference in our lives.

The rules people don't like would tend to be in a city where they don't live. On average, over time, everyone but the un-appeasables would live in a place where the bar was set more in accordance with their liking than it is now. This can only result more freedom. When every county and city is free to set the bar where they will yet still none of them suits you, perhaps the problem is not with them!

I can object to some government practice ultimately by going to the next state or next city. I am not talking about some gross abuse of human rights such as slavery. Under localism the federal government actively prevents slavery because freedom of movement and property is the one right which is federally protected, while other rights are protected by the states. I am referring here to issues like "should it be legal for me to smoke pot" or "should the state recognize homosexual relationships as marriage?" Localism posits that the central government should not have any authority or business pushing the respective states one way or the other on such issues. The central government's inward reach is limited to ensuring freedom of movement of federal citizens and their property claims within its borders.

Just as states would have leeway within the union under localism, counties would have more leeway within the states. Further, if there is a dispute within a large state over such issues, and the fissures are deep enough, counties are free to seek state affiliations more to their liking.

Localism greatly lowers the "transaction costs" of escaping from bad (for you, maybe good to those who stay) government. Decent people will desert indecent government. Thus the market will swiftly punish governments which make rules out of harmony with the moral order of the universe.

Jesus had some very interesting instructions to His disciples regarding government persecution. In the tenth chapter of the Gospel of Matthew He said "When they persecute you in one city, flee to the next." That runs counter to much of our thinking today, where the tendency is to stay and fight. But the wisdom in His counsel is that if it were followed, over time believers would all be in cities which welcomed them and they would be away from those who had a way of doing things that was hostile toward believers.

Over time, whichever group was most in accordance with moral reality would prosper, and the other groups could either adapt or be left out. That is the power of the market at work in respect to government. Modern centralization of power has undermined this important idea so that there is no way to escape persecution and no way to let moral reality assert itself. This is what Localism seeks to change.

In conclusion, perfection is not an option under human government. An unwillingness or inability to accept this reality has led to much human pain and suffering. The utopian idea that if only we imposed this system or that, empowered these people or those, then we could have a perfect society, is just wrong. It operates from a flawed premise about who man is. People are the problem with paradise. There are no perfect people out there to administer one's perfect system.

The best we can hope for is to have a system of checks and balances which creates the right feedback conditions to minimize the injustices which will inevitably arise under human government. As we have discussed, a certain amount of injustice will also exist in the absence of government. If we are successful, the combined injustices of the government will be less than that amount of injustice which would have occurred in that same society absent that government.

Supporters of the central state are very good at taking anecdotal stories of local injustices and using these as example of how indispensable the central state is for keeping localities in line. This is a disguised appeal to emotion enabled by focusing on injustice from one source but ignoring it from another. For every instance of injustice or drop of innocent blood in human history for which a local government is responsible, localists (and anarchists) can point to many times as much which can be laid at the door of the central state.

Systems with many checks and balances are not the most efficient, but they are the most resilient and reliable. Making the market (along with the state governments) the enforcer for the correction of abuses may not always produce results as quickly as the central state in addressing injustices from local authorities, but it will do so in a more reliable and resilient manner. With the central state, some abuses may not be corrected at all, especially those instituted by the central government itself.

The fear that local governments will do something to violate people's rights is probably one of the most common reasons people are slow to accept localism. Local governments will abuse people's rights. That will happen regardless of what system of government one has. So will central governments, if they can. The question is not which system, localism or the central state, will make sure government never violates your rights, because that is a utopian impossibility. Rather the question is under which system is this threat minimized and most easily corrected?

Localism's way of dealing with government's abuse is more subtle than the answers given by the central state, but I would argue they are also more effective. I would compare it to the free market vs. some Soviet-era nations "Five Year Plan" for production. Let's take for example ladies footwear. There is no central government program for making sure the right shoes are produced in the right quantities. There doesn't have to be. Empowering the individual consumer with choice causes that to happen better than any top-down directive from the Federal Government to make good shoes could ever hope to work.

In the same way Localism protects rights in a way which is more subtle, yet more effective, than the false answer from the central state that all will be well if only you give their commissars enough power. This important subject will be discussed in more detail, from a slightly different angle, in the next chapter.

The Central State vs. Localism in Protecting Rights and Producing Liberty

Though this is barely more than a re-phrasing of the prior objection, advocates for the central state sometimes object to the lack of “recourse” to the central enforcement mechanism of a central state under localism. When there is really only one objection that is not pure smoke-screen, you can bet that it will be presented in multiple ways. Because that has happened and will happen, it is worth delving into what is basically the same objection from another angle:

OBJECTION TO LOCALISM: *"In the end, the central state provides a needed recourse against the abuses of petty dictators and misguided moral-crusaders. How would a system of appeals work in localism?"*

ANSWER: First let's get a decent definition of what we mean by the question. Clearly, the objector does not want any of their "rights" violated by the locality. Localists don't either. We would say though, if any government entity was going to violate our rights, we would much prefer it be a local one rather than a state or national one. In such a case it is both easier to remove one’s self out from under the authority of the offending entity, or to successfully fight the abuse and change the policy which prompted it.

Let's start by understanding what rights are. Rights are claims against the majority. They are things an individual is entitled to even if the majority does not approve. In a Republic, such as we once had in the United States, the founding document of the nation, and the states, listed what things they agreed were not subject to a majority vote. Those things were recognized as rights. That's the way we are supposed to still do it now, and that is the way it would be done under localism.

The difference is that for almost all matters, state courts would be responsible for deciding such cases, based on state constitutions. Individuals aggrieved by the actions of a locality appeal to their state courts, except on matters where agents or associates of the state are interfering with their right of exit or property rights in a state which they have exited. Except for such limited circumstances, no one, not even the federal government, would hold that "one ring of power" which is the ability to define, and redefine, rights for the whole nation.

I know that many people have very strong opinions on what their rights are and what things the society in which they live ought to recognize as rights. But I must ask you, why is one's neighbor bound by your view of what your rights ought to be? Your neighbor has not contracted with you to abide by your interpretation of, for example, the non-aggression principle in their interactions with you. They may not even believe in the non-aggression principle as a limit on state action. The only thing they may have agreed to, at least implicitly if they are a citizen, is to abide by the laws as they stand regarding what your rights are.

We may feel the bar should be moved higher. We may very strongly believe that where we want the bar to be set is the place it should be set for all places and all people at all times.

Many moral absolutists have felt just that way about wherever they thought that the bar should be set. My point is that each of us do not get to unilaterally decide that for our neighbors. If they agree to it, then they are obligated to abide by their agreement. It's a contract.

If your neighbor declares that the view of rights which they hold is to be the standard by which your relations will be conducted you might find it high-handed. It doesn't justify collectivism, but this is pretty much how anarchists tend to conduct themselves and its wrong. It is just as much imposing conditions on people without their consent as your neighbors telling you that they and they alone will decide what your rights are.

Just because we think our own moral principles are better than those in which our neighbor believes is no justification to attempt to impose those principles on them against their will. Instead, we use (hopefully) reason to persuade them to agree to our ideas. When broad agreement has been reached among a group of people, the principle becomes enshrined in law. The right becomes recognized. We might mutually agree to declare some areas of life to be the purview of the individual, and not subject to majority vote or regulation by law. They are therefore individual "rights".

Is it not clear that when fifty groups of people each get to decide what our rights (areas of life off-limits to government) are then we will have more areas of freedom overall than when one group in one city decides this? Oh it may be that a group here or there leaves something off that the central authority might include, but for every instance of that we might expect 49 instances of the opposite, that one of the other groups recognized a right that the central authorities were uncomfortable with.

Since we believe in a moral order to the universe, we might expect the areas of freedom recognized by the fifty groups would have considerable overlap with one another, and with whatever areas of freedom the central authority came up with. I would argue that, given a virtuous population, since the fifty groups would be in competition with each other, and the one central government would have no market pressure to conform to conform to moral reality, that the circles of the fifty would be, on average, closer to moral reality than that of the one. For every one of the fifty which conformed less to moral reality, there would be more than one which conformed better.

But even if I am wrong about market pressure producing a better list of recognized rights, just based on the law of averages alone the Localist system will produce more freedom than a central state. Draw a circle on a piece of paper and say it represents the rights recognized by the central state. Then draw fifty circles with slightly different centers which vary in size but are the same average size, as the first circle. The total area of the fifty circles will have greater total area than the first circle. In the same way, a localist nation will have more true rights recognized by the government than will a central state.

Not only that, but the areas which are in and out of each circle will, on average, be more satisfactory to the citizens who live in each state. If some area is left off of one state list which is included in another, then perhaps the reason for it was that this is was not seen as so important to citizens of that state. Where the people think it is important, it will be recognized.

States are not bound to recognize what we think our rights should be, but they *are* bound to recognize what rights are set forth in the compact which established that state- the state constitution. This is the basis of a Republic. The state has contracted with the citizen to set agreed-on areas of life off-limits to its interference. If the central government could not directly impose a list of rights more to your liking under this system, then know also that it could not easily impose one less to your liking either.

In localism the hope that the central government would force all states to do it the way you want is traded for the near certainty that if a state did not do it the way you wanted, you could find another more to your liking. This would not just be because you could move to another state. If your neighbors agreed with you, it would even be possible to transfer your locality to a different state by moving political lines rather than moving people.

In Localism all government relationships from the county up are ultimately voluntary. Counties don't have to stay in a state where their residents feel that their rights are being violated. This market-based approach will make states more deferential to the rights of individual citizens than will a central body which defines and protects "rights". I have spent some time arguing why the Localist approach to defining rights would be better, let me now turn to why the centralized approach to defining rights would be worse.

The hope that those who see things as we do will forever hold the scepter is a vain one. The more concentrated power is then the more attractive a target the power centers become for the ambitious. As with many thrones and palaces throughout history, you might expect it to change owners repeatedly until finally settling in the most ruthless of hands.

When the power to define rights is concentrated in one set of hands with no competition, defending rights may be the stated goal, but not the real goal, of the rights-defining body. A survey of the history of how the modern central state treats its citizens should be sufficient to disabuse the open mind of the notion that empowering a central state to be the sole arbiter of rights would be any guarantee of justice, or even stability.

The more power you put into any one institution, the more attractive a target it becomes for those who want to use it to loot and impose their own will over others. Since "rights" under our system represent things not subject even to majority vote, the power to define "rights" is the power of dictatorship, and the new view is that *groups* can have "rights", not just individuals.

This madness puts politics over justice since the various groups can then form coalitions to seize the rights-defining machinery in order to grant themselves special privileges. Thus the central "justice" system that critics of localism say that we need to protect us from abusive localities becomes itself the primary source of abuse, and one that is much harder to correct (since it is not subject to majority vote anywhere) and much harder to escape (since it applies to the entire nation).

Notice I am not saying that this is not something which *can* happen when the power to define rights is centralized. Rather I am saying it is what has happened, and what *must* eventually happen each and every time you centralize the power to define rights. This unfortunate pattern will repeat until some future age where human nature itself has been altered.

Only by subjecting the power to define rights to competition and the market can one hope to keep this power within its proper boundary of defending the moral order of the universe rather than undermining it. And the plain fact is that humans will have honest disagreements about where the boundaries for "rights" are. There may be only one right answer to that question, but rational people ought to be wary of claims from people who say they know all of those answers for all people for all times.

We grope about darkly along the path to virtue and justice. Illumination often comes in the form of learning from our mistakes and seeing others who have found a way to do things better. That process is short-circuited in a system with a single reference point for defining the outer boundaries of rights.

What recourse is there to potential violations of rights from the state in a localist nation? Suppose for example, Mississippi or South Carolina did something reprehensible such as re-enact Jim Crow laws? Is the only choice of an aggrieved minority in such a case to pack up and leave since the central government only guarantees freedom of property and movement from the states?

Not at all. Maybe if states had as much freedom as Localism permits one might go mad and enact Jim Crow laws. But if counties had as much freedom as localism permits then a large number, perhaps the majority, of counties would either use their ability to lessen the penalty for breaking such "laws" to nothing, or use their right of exit to join some neighboring state, or even form their own state.

It is just really hard to push minorities around when each local unit can cut all ties with a central authority which does something really outrageous. And of course, not all whites in Mississippi would support a return of such laws. Whatever counties were left, after everybody who wanted to could leave, would be so isolated I could see them getting kicked out of the Union. That is the deterrent which comes from making all ties between governmental units from the county up voluntary.

But let's say some population, after all we should have learned, was so intent on pushing Jim Crow laws that they were willing to take the hit on that. Isn't ejecting them from the union the better choice for our nation? Do we really want to stay in political union with such people? Is their assistance in selecting our President and federal representatives really desired or helpful?

States can be kicked out of the union if the other states don't like the way they treat their citizens (after all who want to leave do so, plus parts of the offending state vote to split and stay with the union). Again, this is the short version, and please don't compare it to perfection, compare it to the results we have from the central state concept we have now!

Nothing can guarantee that abuse of rights-definition powers will never occur. Those with faith in Utopian systems make me nervous. But we can make it so these inevitable abuses can be minimized and automatically checked by market forces. At any rate all that I have written above presumes that the typical citizen has at least some measure of virtue. If they do not, then we labor in vain to devise a system of self-government which will produce a happy outcome.

Without some measure of virtue attempts at self-government are futile. We might be just as well off with a dictator or an oligarchy. That is the core position of those who want a centralized rights-recognizing body anyway. They don't trust their neighbors, nor even the leading citizens of their communities so much as they trust some distant elites, some mythical experts, or some media created political personality whom they have never met.

My own view is that I am flawed, my neighbors are flawed, and those who would presume to be our elites are also flawed- perhaps even more flawed than the rest of us. None of us can be trusted with all of the power to define rights, that is why it too, it especially, must be dispersed.

The Conclusion of Things

"*The most basic question is not 'what is best?' but 'who shall decide what is best?'*" - Thomas Sowell

****

Many theories and philosophies and ideas about government have been conceived of in the course of mankind's journey. In the end though, it is either going to be Localism or Globalism. This is so because, if for no other reason, no other philosophy of government contains within it the means to protect a society from the centralization of government power which must end in globalism.

Either societies, left, right, or center, will adopt the protections endorsed in *Localism, a philosophy of government*, or they will find that the answer to the question of "who decides what is best?" will be continually moved farther away from the individual citizen over time. In the history of America we have seen that each generation has lived with a government more centralized, with more decisions moved farther from the input of the individual, than each generation beforehand. This is not chance, it is not by accident. It is not something that just happened as a result of bad luck or misfortune. It is what *must* happen in a stable society unless specific and comprehensive measures are taken to prevent it.

When Thomas Jefferson said “God forbid we should ever be twenty years without such a rebellion” he understood that stability in government leads to a loss of freedom. He viewed instability as a price worth paying to keep government the servant of the citizens rather than their master. Localism attempts to achieve the same end by substituting the tension of market competition to check government in place of rebellion.

Because Localism can accommodate much of the broad middle of the political spectrum, its opposition must come from the extremes. One extreme end of the spectrum is commitment to the central state. Most of mankind is presently suffering under this extreme. At the other end of the spectrum can be found those who are in constant rebellion against all government- not as a measure to keep government accountable to individual citizens, but against government in principle.

Early on the book discussed why people hold these extreme views of government, and how and why much of the divide is along a generational fault line. The young and old have a very different view of the relative danger of Public Threats vs. Private Threats to liberties. These divergent views, while each based on a certain aspect of reality, are both out of balance.

A great deal of space was devoted to answering arguments from the more inflexible end of the Libertarian/Anarchist spectrum. These answers were divided into two main parts: 1) Why the premises behind such thought are not necessarily true in theory, and 2) Why societies built around them have not and cannot work in practice.

The key idea behind the first part is that if there is a God then it is not reasonable to suppose that the powers of government flow solely from individual persons. There is in such a case a Divine Moral Order, and governments which conform to it come closer to reflecting moral reality than governments based on views of government which make it a purely human institution. In such a case government does not reflect merely a delegation of powers from individual persons, but rather operate, as scripture taught and Western civilization believed, as God's ministers to serve people by upholding justice.

The other premise one could take is that there is no God. In such a case though, one should not expect others to agree to the Non-Aggression Principle or in Delegation and Symmetry as limits to government power. This is because without a Divine reference point for morality those choices become no more or less valid than any other choice about what government might be like.

Perhaps someone else believes that the strong should rule the weak, that the smart should rule the obtuse, that one race should rule another. Why are they wrong? Because the anarchist says so? Without a reference point outside of mankind no one choice can be said to be more "right" or "wrong" than another, only that you might have an individual preference for one choice over another.

The second part went into some detail about why anarchist ideas, and for that matter more absolutist shades of Libertarianism, cannot be sustained in practice. Basically such a society cannot protect itself from large central states. This is true in the most direct sense of military conquest but even more so in regards to the corrupting influence of fiat money. Some choices are good for the individual and that right soon, but bad for society as a whole in the course of time. If there is no government to limit or sanction such actions, they will over time lead to the end of individual freedom. The use of fiat currency, even that of other nations, is one such course of action.

“Heavens List of Rights” is not an easy subject. Those of us conditioned to want the “one right answer” (and that in two minutes) may have needed some patience to get through that one. The short answer, as short as I can make it, is that the amount of freedom, the amount of life off-limits to government which a society can have without shaking apart into chaos, is dependent on the virtue of the population. Systems of government, localism included, cannot fix that problem-one can't invent a system of government so perfect that it will work even if the people are immoral. Self-Government merely gives the wicked the power to get themselves in trouble. It is then they will either cry out to a tyrant to restore order or cry out to God to save their souls, In that sense, freedom is ultimately evangelical. No wonder so many dread it.

Lastly, I addressed the issue of the central state. I had no need to go into what is wrong with the central state, for its flaws are all around us. Rather I commented on the types of people who tend to support it. Some of them can be persuaded, but other mind-sets are not interested in being persuaded. It's a waste of your time trying to persuade them. Your energies are better spent attempting to *defeat* them by the measures outlined in the third pillar of *Localism, a philosophy of government.*

There was one attempt at a rational argument which adherents for a central state have made against Localism. That is that it would permit more injustice locally than we now have. Once can always trade anecdotes about local abuses vs. those of central governments, but a logical comparison of the two forms shows that there must be more freedom in a localist society than there is in a central state.

I would like to conclude by thanking my readers for caring enough about what is true to finish a work of this nature; non-frivolous; low on cute stories; requiring much thought to read. Not everyone in a nation must know the things contained here and in the first book, *Localism a philosophy of government*, for that nation to remain free, but some must know them. Thank you for taking the trouble to make yourself one of those who know.

THE END

Thank You for Your Patronage!

We invite you to read the original book on Localism from Mark: "Localism, a Philosophy of Government".

Also, be on the lookout for Mark's foray into theology: "Early Genesis, the Revealed Cosmology".

Mark has also written a novella that is historical fiction set in the First World War- "Thorns of the Rose" as well as a modern adaptation of an American Folk-tale - "John Henry". Those are e-books designed to be short, fun reads.

In addition, Mark edited a little gift-book designed to be a graduation gift for churches or church schools to give to their graduates called "Senior Graduation".

www.ingramcontent.com/pod-product-compliance
Lightning Source LLC
Chambersburg PA
CBHW032110280326
41933CB00009B/782

9780996239004